A NARRATIVE OF A JOURNEY FROM CAUNPOOR TO THE BOORENDO PASS IN THE HIMALAYA MOUNTAINS

A Narrative of a Journey from Caunpoor to the Boorendo Pass in the Himalaya Mountains

VIA

GWALIOR, AGRA, DELHI, AND SIRHIND

1821-22

WILLIAM LLOYD

AND

ALEXANDER GERARD'S

ACCOUNT OF AN ATTEMPT TO PENETRATE BY BEKHUR TO GARO AND THE LAKE MANASAROWARA

1821

WITH A MAP

Edited by

GEORGE LLOYD

IN TWO VOLUMES

VOLUME ONE

MANOHAR

2022

First published 1840
Reprinted 2022

ISBN 978-93-91928-53-7 (Vol. 1)
ISBN 978-93-91928-69-8 (Set)

Published by
Ajay Kumar Jain *for*
Manohar Publishers & Distributors
4753/23 Ansari Road, Daryaganj
New Delhi 110 002

Printed at
Replika Press Pvt. Ltd.

NARRATIVE

OF A

JOURNEY FROM CAUNPOOR

TO THE

BOORENDO PASS IN THE HIMALAYA MOUNTAINS,

Viâ GWALIOR, AGRA, DELHI, AND SIRHIND:

BY

MAJOR SIR WILLIAM LLOYD.

AND

CAPTAIN ALEXANDER GERARD'S

ACCOUNT OF AN ATTEMPT TO PENETRATE BY BEKHUR TO GAROO, AND THE LAKE MANASAROWARA:

WITH A

LETTER

FROM THE LATE

J. G. GERARD, Esq.

DETAILING A

Visit to the Shatool and Boorendo Passes,

FOR THE PURPOSE OF DETERMINING THE LINE OF PERPETUAL SNOW ON THE SOUTHERN FACE OF THE HIMALAYA, &c., &c., &c.

With Maps.

EDITED BY GEORGE LLOYD.

VOL. I.

J. MADDEN & Co.,

(Late Parbury & Co.)

8, LEADENHALL STREET.

1840.

TO

SIR RICHARD JENKINS, G.C.B., M.P.,

CHAIRMAN OF THE HON. THE COURT OF DIRECTORS

OF THE

EAST INDIA COMPANY.

SIR,

I look up to you, from more than ordinary circumstances, as a friend. My father commanded your body-guard for many years, when you were the representative of the British Government at the Court of the Rajah of Berar, in which time I was born, as it were, in your family. It was also during that eventful period that you performed the highest public services, for which Her Majesty has lately conferred on you a most merited distinction. I have since been able to appreciate those services, and, moreover, have had the pleasure, not to say honour, of receiving from you much kindness. Accept this work, therefore, as a slight testimony of the sincere admiration and esteem of—

SIR,

Your obliged and humble Servant,

G. LLOYD.

Brynestyn, February 1, 1840.

EDITOR'S PREFACE.

It was with pleasure that I undertook the task of editing these volumes; I finish it in sorrow. But private grief is no subject for public information, and it will therefore be sufficient for me to say, that the valued author of the "Account of an Attempt to Penetrate by Bekhur to Garoo and the Lake Manasarowara," Captain Alexander Gerard, is now no more. From the fatigues he had for many years undergone, together with a fever, which since his return to England has periodically attacked him, his frame and constitution were shattered. It is only two or three months since that he had the usual return of his malady; but still he did not apprehend any immediate danger until the 12th of December, when he became alarmingly unwell, and expired in his native town of Aberdeen, on the 15th, having been only three days seriously ill.

To speak in praise of the living too often, resembles flattery, but no such imputation can be attached when we render justice to those who are voiceless to the interests of this world. In the preface I had formerly written I had attempted to render justice to the merits of one brother, and little then did I dream, that the same paragraph would enclose both! Yet what can be said?

This is no place for a biography. I must therefore beg the candid reader to form his own esti mation of my late friends from their productions. I feel a confidence in saying so, for I am sure that he will accord them that fame, that general fame, which is so justly their due.

The late Captain Alexander Gerard corrected his Narrative purposely for this work, as it had formerly appeared merely in scraps, and imperfect. It is therefore an authentic document. The letter from the late J. G. Gerard, Esq. was written upon the spot, and contains facts and results of much importance upon the Isothermal lines of the Himalaya mountains.

I have to thank my publishers, Messrs. Madden and Co., for the very handsome manner in which they have, to use a technical expression, "got up" the work, as well as for affording me every assistance in their power to facilitate the progress of these volumes. This may seem trifling to those unaccustomed to printing, but it is well known to be a point of the utmost importance to those who are aware of its many impediments and difficulties.

I have now, to the best of my abilities, discharged my trust. It is foi opinion and time to decide for or against those for whose reputation I have willingly laboured.

GEORGE LLOYD.

Brynestyn, January 1, 1840.

Table of Contents

Vol. I

BOOK I.

MAJOR SIR WILLIAM LLOYD'S NARRATIVE.

"It seemed to me *requisite*, that the loftiest subjects should be treated of in language more than usually elevated. To have written in colder terms, would have argued either want of capacity, or, what I should think far more degrading, have rendered me suspected of insensibility."—*Maurice's Indian Antiquities, preface, page* 65.

INTRODUCTION.

As I think that the following Narrative combines instruction with amusement, I take the responsibility of presenting it to the public. I use the word "Public," in its most extended sense, for I am aware that, many of the facts relating to the Himalaya, contained in it, have already appeared in three separate publications, as well as in the Transactions of a learned body, (besides various ephemeral productions,) all of which are familiar to those who have the means of procuring such expensive works. The mass of readers, however, I conclude, are wholly ignorant of this extraordinary country and its sublimity, and it is to the *mass* rather than the favoured few, although they will find in it much that is authentically novel to them, that I offer the result, not only of my own personal observation, but that also of my late valued and enterprising friends Captain Alexander Gerard, of the Bengal Army, and J. G. Gerard, Esq., of the Bengal Medical Establishment.

During my journey I kept a diary, in which I carefully noted down every thing that appeared to me worthy of observation, as well as the feelings which the singular and magnificent aspect of nature excited under all the varied circumstances of storm, serenity, and danger.

Since my return to England this journal has been almost the class-book of my son, who has elucidated it by numerous historical notices of the cities we passed through on the plains. He accompanied me as far as Koteghur, where, from his youth and the difficulties of the further progress, I left him. We have since rambled together through Switzerland, and, as he is from these circumstances, but more particularly from his literary attainments, better qualified than I am to prepare my journal for publication, I have intrusted the task to him with confidence. Not a single paragraph, however, has been allowed to go to press without having been most carefully considered by me.

Thus much I have, as a lover of truth, and from a sense of duty to the public, thought it necessary to state: more would be superfluous.

WILLIAM LLOYD.

Brynestyn, January 1, 1840.

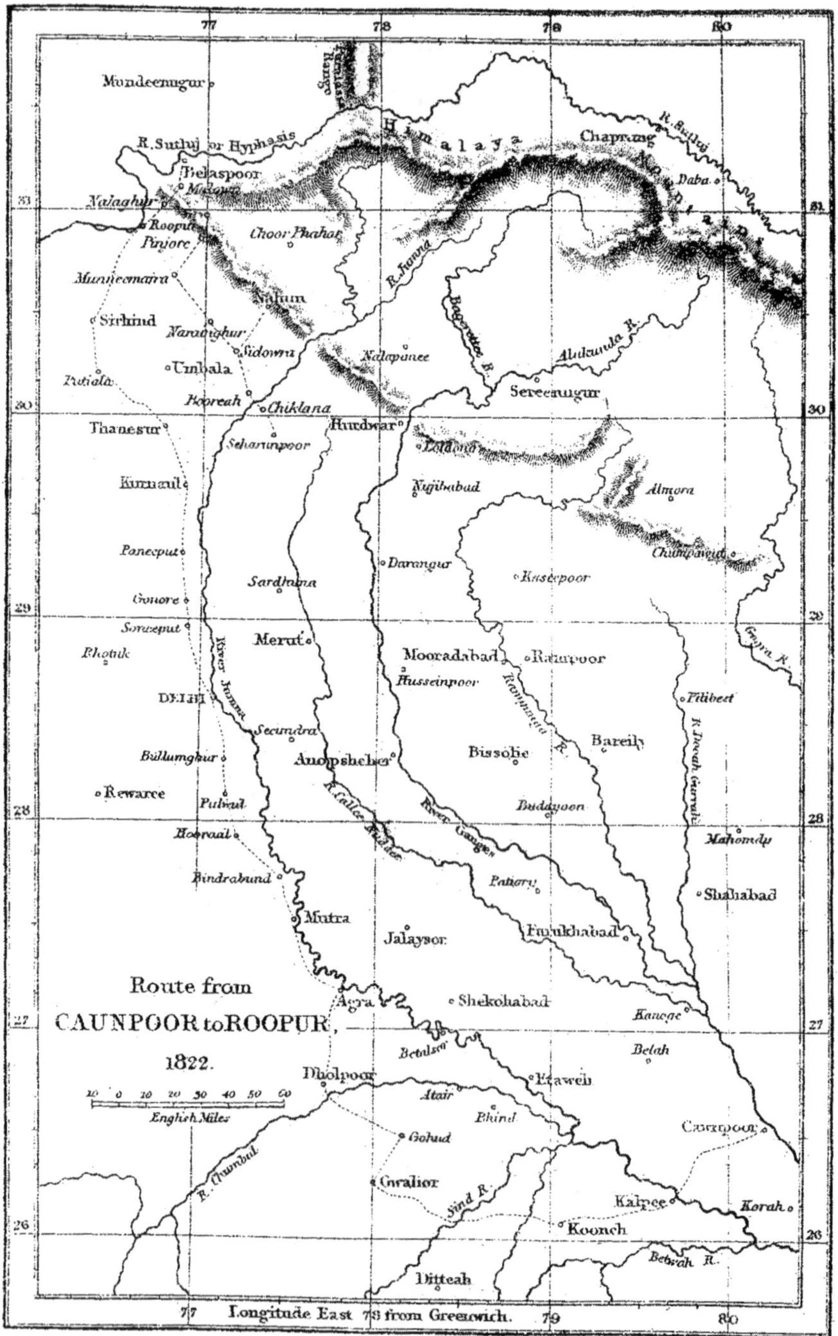

London. J. Madden. & Co. 1840.

Engraved by J. & C. Walker

BOOK I.

CHAPTER I.

NARRATIVE FROM CAUNPOOR TO KURNAUL.

Caunpoor is a military cantonment stretching some miles along the right bank of the Ganges. It is in N. lat. 26° 28′ 23″, E. long. 80° 13′, and is distant from Calcutta 638 miles by the road in a W.N.W. direction. Forty years since it was a place of great importance from its advanced position, as well as its proximity to the Soobah* of Oude; but

* "I shall now proceed to give the substance of what we find in the Ayeen Akbery, relative to the greater and smaller divisions of Hindostan, as fixed by the Emperor Acbar, in the fortieth year of his reign, that is, about the year 1595 of the Christian Æra. * * * *."

"Hindostan was then parcelled out into twelve grand divisions called Soobahs, to each of which a viceroy was assigned, by the title of Soobahdar, corruptly written Soobah by European writers, for Soobah signifies province: many now we see our squadrons encamped on the banks of the Sutluj, 480 miles further to the N. W., within a few marches of the far famed Hyphasis, which was the limit of the Indian conquest under Alexander.

I left Caunpoor on the 22nd December, 1821, and crossing the Doab, arrived at Kalpee on the 3rd of January, having loitered on the road to give my son the advantage of change of air.

Kalpee is a large town built in the midst of ravines, and bordering the right shore of the Jumna, for about two miles. It was the capital of a Sircar* during the Mahummedan Government. Its remains of former opulence are confined to mausoleums, and simple tombs, which are very

---

of these Soobahs were in extent equal to large European kingdoms. The Soobahs were again divided into Circars, which Mr. Rennel would call counties; and these were subdivided into purgunnahs, which he would call hundreds. The names of the twelve Soobahs were Allahabad, Agra, Owdh, Ajmere, Ahmed-abad, Bahar, Bengal, Dehly, Cabul, Lahoor, Multan, and Malwa. When Accar conquered Berar, Khandeess, and Ahmednagur, they were formed into three Soobahs, increasing the number to fifteen."—*Maurice's Indian Antiquities*, vol. 1, part 1, c. III, p. 94. London. Richardson.

* See the foregoing note.

numerous on the outside of the town. I counted thirty domes of mausoleums, but there was only one of any size. Although there are many trees in the town, there are very few in the surrounding country, which, together with the numerous sepulchres gives Kalpee a desolate appearance.

A great quantity of cotton is brought here from the countries westward of the Jumna, and is sent down from hence by water to Calcutta.

The country between Caunpoor and Kalpee is level and well cultivated, but it contains little to interest the traveller.

On the 14th January, I continued my journey to Gwalior.

14th January, *Attah,* 10m. 2f. The road good. This is a large village.

15th January, *Ooriee,* 11m. 2f. Road like yesterday's. A large village with a Gurhee.* We got our water from a fine tank and rivulet. Halted the 16th.

17th January, *Hirdoee,* 10m. 1f. A moderate village defended by a good gurhee. The villagers are in comfortable circumstances.

* The general name for a fort.

18th January, *Koanch,* 9m. 4f. This is a large commercial town. We pitched our tents beside a good tank. The fort here is in ruins. It appears to me an oblong of 200 paces by 175, and seems never to have been strong.

Between Kalpee, and Koanch, the country is quite flat, and very highly cultivated, producing an abundance of cotton. Saltpetre is found in small quantities in the neighbourhood.

19th January, *Nuddeegaon,* 12m. A small town, with a fort, on the right bank of the Poohauj river, belonging to the Rajah of Dutteeah. The Poohauj is a clear stream, a circumstance which I should not mention, but that it is the first clear stream I have seen since leaving Caunpoor.

This place like Kalpee is situated amongst ravines, through which we wound for three miles before we reached the town. Excellent Chinnerees are made here. They are a pretty kind of cloth, dyed with bright and permanent colours.

20th January, halted.

21st January, *Aswar,* 11m. 4f. A small village belonging to Holkar. After quitting Nuddeegaon we ascended out of the ravines, and then traversing a low jungle for about a mile, came upon a flat country which was interspersed with woods and cultivation. We passed by the villages of Tola, and Ukdeo on the route.

22nd January, *Sehura,* 6m. 4f. Sehura is a considerable town on the right bank of the Sind river. It contains good markets, and is in a flourishing state. The fort which is on the river side, is large, and built of brick and stone. It has several guns on the ramparts, but its position is bad, the ravines running up to the ditch, and outer wall in several places, which present favourable points of attack. There is a beautiful view here. The Sind falls over a ledge of rocks into a spacious basin, in three separate cascades. In this ledge are some ancient excavations which contain images of Gunnais* and Mahadeo, believed

* "We find that it was the peculiar office of Ganesa (Gunnais) to present to the Deity all the oblations, and all the devout addresses of mankind to their Creator. The elephant's head is the emblem of sagacity, and he is styled the god of prudence and policy. Hence even worldly business of any importance is always commenced by an ejaculation to Ganesa, and he is invoked at the beginning of most Indian books, an instance of which occurs in the Heetopades, translated by Mr. Wilkins, which opens with, 'Reverence

by the credulous Hindoos, to be the work of their Gods.* Over these sanctuaries the water rolls like a veil of gossamer woven with diamonds. On the right shore are several large buildings occupied by Byraggies,† and beyond them is the fort upon an

---

to Ganesa.' "—*Maurice's Indian Antiquities*, Dissert. 2, p. 250. London. Richardson.

* "If ever, on the other hand, the dreadful attributes of the destroying god, Mahadeo, were accurately pourtrayed, are they not evident in the monstrous, distorted, and terrific features of the remaining aspect? The eyebrows of that face are contracted into frowns, the skin of the nose is drawn upwards, and the *alce nostri* distended, expressing contempt and indignation. The face, too, is darkened by whiskers, which the others have not, and the tongue is violently thrust out between the teeth. The right hand of this dreadful figure grasps a large hooded snake, which it holds aloft and surveys with a stern look. * * * * Another hand which is now broken off, appears to have had a snake of the same hooded and enormous kind."—*Maurice's Indian Antiquities*, Dissert. 2, p. 248. London. Richardson.

† The Byraggies are sectaries of Vishnu, and distinguish themselves by two stripes of yellow ochre, or sandal upon their foreheads, and a string of Tulsi beads round their necks. They profess to be exempt from human passions, and are therefore like other Fakeers or holy mendicants, supposed to know orisons which are especially efficacious in cases of sterility in women. The following is the derivation.

" Berag, comprehending and despising the things of this

elevated spot. On the left is a low range of rocky eminences which, with the town, temples, and precipitous sides of the river, complete the graceful picture.

This place is in the possession of the Dutteeah Rajah, whose hospitality I shall ever remember. He kindly permitted me to shoot in his chace, and furnished me besides, with horsemen, and Shecarries* to beat up the game. I killed a Nil Gau,† and wounded another, which, notwithstanding the sharp pursuit of the horsemen that were with me, escaped.

Halted the 23rd and 24th January.

---

world."—*Ayeen Akbery.* Translated *by Gladwin*, v. 3. *Expla. of some Sanscrit words.* See also the *Dissertation*, p. xxxvii. to *Dows' History of Hindostan*, v. 1.

* "The Shecarrie is a free occupation open to all religions and classes; though ordinarily its followers are not very remarkable for morality or sobriety. Nevertheless, they seem to possess a certain portion of esteem among the inhabitants around them, and being in many respects useful, are rather protected than discouraged. They are generally excellent in their profession, being good marksmen, and very expert in various kinds of poaching They study the habits, and are well acquainted with the seasons of every species of game, of which they destroy vast quantities."—*Williamson's Oriental Field Sports.*

† Antilope picta Gm.

25th January, *Rutwah,* 9m. 4f. Forded the Sind, and crossed over stony hills to Durrowlee about six miles from Sehura. It is the last village belonging to the Dutteeah Rajah. The aspect of the country has changed and become wilder. My baggage carts were six hours on the road.

Rutwah is a village with a small gurhee belonging to Scindiah. A rivulet of clear water runs by our tents.

26th January, *Behut,* 9m. 4f. For the first mile the route lay over stony eminences, and then was for the rest of the day good. At 4m. 4f. passed Rungawun, a place where some of Scindiah's Mahratta horsemen were stationed. Rungawun, and Behut are inconsiderable villages, defended by small stone forts.

The villages are now built of stone. At this place is an old fort called Chutterghur, situated among some low hills, which contains a very handsome house, now in ruins, built by the Rana* of Gohud.

Halted during the 27th and 28th, expecting letters from Major Close, the representative of our Government, at the court of Scindiah.

* Rana, Raja, Race, Prince.

29th January, *Soonee,* 17m. The route good. Soonee is a small place about 1m. 2f. westward of Beejowlee.

30th January, *Gwalior,* 12 miles. Arrived at the Residency to breakfast.

The town of Gwalior lies around the northern, and eastern side of the insulated rock upon which the fortress stands. It is large, built of stone, and contains about 50,000 inhabitants. There is a handsome mosque in it, and a beautiful mausoleum which covers the remains of Mahummed Gous. Within the same enclosure is the tomb of the celebrated musician Tan Sein, who was the delight of Ackbar's court. Close by it is a small tree, the leaves of which impart when chewed a heavenly harmony to the voice. This is religiously believed by all dancing girls.* On the eastern side

* "His voice was as sweet as if he had chewed the leaves of that enchanted tree, which grows over the tomb of the musician, Tan Sein."—*Lalla Rookh.*

"We were in such spirits, and so delighted with their songs and performance, that had Tansain been present at that hour he would have forgot his strains." And in the note to this is added, "Tansain and Bawurra are worshipped by singers and musical performers."—*The Tale of the Four Durwesh,* p. 28.

of the hill are a great number of figures of Boodh,* from twenty-five to thirty feet in height, cut out of the solid rock which forms a recess around them.

The celebrated fortress of Gwalior, is upon the long flat insulated hill I have already mentioned, which is about 3 or 400 yards in breadth, and a mile, and a half in length. The highest part of it is said to be 450 feet above the plain. It runs almost north, and south. This rock is in most parts inaccessible, and is surmounted by a stone rampart along its edge. The present entrance to

* " Question VII.—Who is Buddha? Is he God or the Creator, or a prophet, or saint; born of heaven, or of a woman?

Answer.—Buddha means, in Sanscrit, the wise; also that which is known by wisdom; and it is one of the names which we give to God, whom we also call A' di-Buddha, because he was before all, and is not created, but is the Creator; and the Pancha Buddhas were created by him, and are in the heavens. Sákya, and the rest of the seven human Buddhas are earth-born or human. These latter by the worship of Buddha, arrived at the highest eminence, and attained Nirvána Pad (i. e. were absorbed into A' di-Buddha). We therefore call them all Buddhas."—*Sketch of Buddhism, derived from the Bauddha Scriptures of Nipal.* By B. H. Hodgson, Esq., M. R. A. S. Trans. R. A Society, vol. 2, p. 238. Parbury & Co., 1830.

it is on the eastern face, but formerly there was one also upon the western, now walled up. This spot might perhaps be easily laid open by artillery, and afford a ready way into the interior of the fort. It is about 200 or 300 paces from the northern point of the hill, and immediately to the south of some gigantic images of Boodh, which occupy three recesses in the rock, distinctly visible from the Residency, the quarter of the British Embassy. The fort of Gwalior was, during the government of the Mogul emperors, the royal prison.*

During my stay I was presented to Dowlut Rao Scindiah, the adopted son of the well known Madhajee Scindiah. He resides here in the midst of his camp in preference to Oojein, which is the capital of his dominions. He is about 43 years of age, dark, short of stature, and of a pleasing address.

The month of February was passed in visiting Gohud, and Behut, and in completing our preparations for our excursion into the Himalaya.

On the 27th of February, my friend Major Close,

* "Bernier's History of the late Revolution of the Empire of Mogol," vol. 1, p. 240, et seq. London 1671.

and myself, sent off our baggage, and tents to Dunela, a small place near Moorabad, which is a little town on the Sunk river, with orders to go on to Hingowna, and there wait for us.

1st March, *Hingowna,* 26m. 3f. To-day we joined our Camp. On our route we forded the Sunk, the Kohar, and another river. At Moorabad there is a bridge of several arches, now in ruins. The road was good, and lay through a well cultivated country.

2nd March, near *Dholpoor,* 13m. 3f. We encamped to-day near the Rana of Dholpoor's residence, which is about three miles west of the town of the same name, in order that we might conveniently visit him in the evening, for it was so much out of our direct way.

The road was good enough till we came to Choolaseraee at the entrance of the extensive ravines, which are characteristic of the vicinity of the Chumbul river. It then became narrow, and winding, but still passable for carriages. These ravines are singular phenomena, and it would not be an easy matter to account for them. Their sides are from twenty to thirty feet high, and appear like a succession of solid waves. They are infested by wolves, hyænas, and jackalls.

We crossed the Chumbul, in rude boats opposite the Fort of Dholpoor, which is situated on a high bank of the river surrounded by ravines, and of little strength. The stream is at this season of the year perhaps 300 yards bıoad, but there is a ford a couple of miles lower down.

Dholpoor has evidently been a place of consequence, judging by the remains of buildings scattered about. It still contains many substantial houses, and its markets are well supplied.

In the evening we visited the Rana, and found him in a wooden bungala* of three or four stories, which takes to pieces, and can be removed from place to place upon carts. He is a talkative old man of sixty at least, and to receive us he had formed a durbar† of a few of his principal attendants, and when we took leave offered us Kheluts,* in short assumed the importance of an independent prince. He was during the Mahratta war of 1803, Rana

* House.

† Durbar, court or levee.

‡ The khelut is a dress of honour, in general a rich one, presented by superiors to inferiors. In the zenith of the

of Gohud, at the conclusion of which Scindiah having claimed Gohud and Gwalior by virtue of the treaty he had formed with the British, they were after much discussion allowed him, and the Rana had Dholpoor assigned to him as a compensation. He is a Jaut,* and has recently married a young girl, by whom he expects offspring, and is therefore very anxious to abolish the horrible custom of female infanticide, so universally prevalent in his tribe. He told us that he could, and would abolish it in his country, if the neighbouring States would follow his example, and had already in order to induce them to do so, sent a Vakeel† to Scindiah. He related to us that

---

Moghul empire these kheluts were expensive honors, as the receivers were obliged to make rich presents to the Emperors for the kheluts they received.—Note 77 to the "*Tale of the Four Durwesh*," p. 23.

* The Játs are Hindús of a low tribe, who, taking advantage of the decline of the Moghul empire, have, by their courage and enterprise, raised themselves into some consequence on the north-western parts of Hindostan, and many of the strongest forts of that part of India are still in their possession.—*Sir J. Malcolm's Sketch of the Sikhs*, p. 136 note. London, Murray, 1812.

† Wukeel, ambassador, envoy, agent, deputy.

every female child was put to death immediately after birth, and that the practice originated from the Emperor Jehaungree taking by force to his bed the young women of this, and other Raujpoot tribes. When these people marry, they select wives from other tribes.

3rd March, *Muneeah,* 9m. 4f.—This is a town of about a thousand houses situated in a fine country. The line of march has become very sandy, and I believe it has nearly the same character as far as Delhi. It is nevertheless better wooded than that portion to the south of the Chumbul.

4th March, *Terah,* 12 m. 6 f.—Terah is a small village in the Company's territory. The boundary is the Bangunga river, which we forded at Jajow-Ka-Seraee, a curious old Mahummedan place. There is a very good Seraee* at Jajow, an

* Serai or Caravanserai are buildings for travellers and merchants in cities, and on the great roads in Asia. Those in Upper Hindostan, built by the Emperors of Dhailee, are grand and costly; they are either of stone or burnt bricks. In Persia they are mostly of bricks dried in the sun. In Upper Hindostan they are commonly twenty miles distant from each other, which is a munzil or stage. They are

elegant Baolee,* and a beautiful pavilion in a garden, all built of red sandstone brought from the quarries at Futteepoor Sicri. There is also a stone bridge here of 20 arches, 270 yards in length, and 10 in breadth. The road over it is flagged, and on a line parallel with the horizon, unlike the generality of bridges in England which form an angle in the centre. The river now, winds along another course, and the bridge is useless. Jajow is remarkable as having been the scene of two decisive battles. The first fought on the 8th June, 1658, in which Aurungzeeb defeated his brother, Dara Shecoh, and the second on the 19th June, 1707, between the son, and grandson of Aurungzeeb Shah Allum, and Azim Ushaun, in which the latter was defeated and slain.†

---

generally a square, with rooms for goods, men and beasts. *The Tale of the Four Durwesh.* Note 162, p. 111.

* Baolee, a well.

† Vide "Hamilton's Description of Hindostan." There is also an account of the first action in 1658, in "Dow's History of Hindostan, v. 3, p. 232, et seq., and one also of the same in "Bernier's History of the late Revolution, &c.," v. 1, p. 102, et seq. London, 1671. Bernier's account is excellent. Indeed few travellers have surpassed Bernier either in descriptive powers or judgment.

5th March, *Agra*, 13 m. 2 f.—During our route we saw another fine old bridge, under which a considerable river had once passed. Its bed is now dry, though during the rains a stream may be formed, but then, a couple of arches would suffice for that which had formerly required fifteen. Between Dholpoor and Agra the country is level, highly cultivated, and well wooded.

Agra is so well known that I need not enter into any description of it. Bernier who lived in it, whilst in its magnificence, will give every desired information, with his usual simplicity and eloquence,* yet to withhold all mention of the Tauj Mahal, the most beautiful mausoleum in the world would be tantamount to a sin. I had visited it last year during a ramble to Hurdwar, and its large aerial dome of white marble, its graceful minarets, and stately body of the same costly material, its garden filled with flowers, and orange and citron trees, its lines of elegant

* "Bernier's Travels". A Letter to Monsieur de la Mothe le Vayer, written at Delhi, July 1st, 1663, containing the description of Delhi and Agra, &c.

fountains, and its majestic gateway had delighted me, and realised what I should otherwise have supposed an impossibility. But this evening I was more than ever charmed with it. The moon's fullest radiance showered over the exquisite marble edifice, the trees were shadowy, and dark, and waved noiselessly in the perfumed wind, the ranges of fountains seemed like the delicate plumes of Egrets, and diffused throughout a delicious coolness; while the silence of the night was only broken at intervals by the solemn recitations from the Koraun by the Moollahs* in the alcoves of the shrine, to the memory of an Empress, aye, more than an empress, a good wife. The poor poet indeed might have raised in his imagination such a structure of perfection to the object of his departed loved One, but only the boundless profusion of treasure by a monarch fresh in grief for the loss of her who

* Moollahs are Doctors of Law as well as Divinity in conformity to the Koran, which legislates equally in temporal as well as spiritual matters. Further information regarding Moollahs may be found in the masterly work of the Hon. M. Elphinstone, upon Caubul, vol. 1, b. 2, c. v. London, Bentley, 1839.

made royalty to him a pleasure, could have commanded the reality of the Tauj Mahal. And where now are the busy multitudes that were gathered here by the munificence of the widowed Shah Jehaun? Where the Omrahs* who were the splendour of his imperial court? Where his glorious, and glittering hosts of soldiers? Where the Emperor himself, the descendant of the famed Timur? All, all dust! like his beloved Moomtaz i Zemani "the most Exalted of the age," over whom he raised this admirable sepulchre, and by whom now, he, and his greatness sleep. The excellence of this tomb has been its talisman. Man has respected it. The ruthless factions that have almost extirpated the race of Timur and Hoomayoon, and their cities, have reverenced it. Even Time, has left unblemished this incomparable work, as though loth to touch a memorial,

* "Omrah is the plural of Emeer, which signifies prince, and is a title given to all the nobility of the first rank in the Moghul empire, and in Tartary."—*Ayeen Akbery*, Translated by Gladwin, vol. 1st, index, ad vocem.—Calcutta, 1783.

sacred to the purest of human sentiments, affection!*

6th March, *Nurkutta,* 10 m. 4 f.—Nurkutta is a small village in a pleasant country, about two miles from Gowghaut on the Jumna. We passed through the town of Agra, and over heaps of ruins, till we arrived at Secundra, where the great Acbar is buried. From the terrace of his mausoleum here, when looking towards his favourite city of Agra, the mind fills with sorrow at beholding for miles the shattered remains of once beautiful palaces, mosques, seraees, baths, gardens, and all that power, accompanied by wealth and luxury, could create, strewed upon the plain, the haunt of lizards, bats, and owls. The morality, however, which such a scene of desolation teaches, is of that austere nature which is known as "the vanity of vanities, all is vanity." Such reflexions would lead to misanthrophy, and I doubt much if that may be termed morality which induces such a sentiment, Still we felt our pity excited in seeing these remains

* Dow's History of Hindostan, vol. 3, p. 141. London, Becket and De Hondt, 1772.

of the chivalrous Acbar's glory. Little more than two centuries have passed, and it has come to this!

7th March, *Furrah,* 12 m.—The road not so heavy, and sandy as yesterday. This is a small town.

8th March, *Muttra,* 13 m. 4 f.—This march has brought us, as if by magic, from the influence of the laws of Mahummed to those of the wise Menu.* The change is indeed striking. Yesterday the "Prophet," and the Moghul emperors were lords paramount, to-day Krishna, the beloved god of the Hindoo women.†

* Menu is regarded by the Hindoos as their wisest and most sacred lawgiver. His "Institutes" are supposed by Sir W. Jones to have been written about 880 years before the Christian æra—*Institutes of Hindu Law.* Calcutta, 1796. Preface, p. vii.

† Kishen Owtar. Above four thousand years ago, Ogur Sein of the Jadown tribe, reigned at Mehtrah, but was dethroned by his son Kenns, who assumed the Government, &c. * * * Kishen was born in the prison at Mehtrah. * * * Kishen in his ninth year killed Kenns, and then restored Ogur Sein to his kingdom. He lived one hundred and five years. He had 16,108 wives, every one of whom brought him ten sons and one daughter. And every wife thought she possessed the whole of Kishen's affections."—*Ayeen Akbery,* v. 2, p. 239, et seq.

Muttra is a very ancient city (supposed to be the Methora of Pliny*) situated on the right bank of the Jumna. It is held in great veneration by the Hindoos as the birth-place of Krishna. The streets are narrow, the houses high, and many of them are large, and massive. It is also celebrated for beautiful women, of whom a class called the Chowbuns bear off the prize from the rest.

Mahmood of Ghizni, having heard Muttra renowned for riches, and sanctity (strange brothers) attacked, and plundered it in 1018, A.D. The wealth he got here was enormous.† He would have destroyed also in his pious zeal the splendid temples, but that he found the task both laborious, and expensive. The place was however ruined, and fell to decay, yet such is the power of faith among the Hindoos, that it was rebuilt, and many

---

Khrisna is the Indian Apollo, and is also called Vishnu. In the Hindoo triad Vishnu represents the preservative power.

* "Maurice's Indian Antiquities," pt. 3, c. 2, p. 375, et seq.

† "Dow's History of Hindostan," v. 1, p. 57.

new temples arose, the most magnificent of which was that erected by Beer Sing Des, Rajah of Oorcha, which cost 36 lacs of rupees.* Aurungzeeb razed it to the ground, and with the materials founded a mosque on the same spot. To complete the history of this town, Ahmed Shah Abdaullee in 1756 inflicted a general massacre on the inhabitants.

We visited whilst here the ex-Paishwa Bajee Rao, and afterwards went to see the Observatory built by Rajah Jysing in the so called old fort near the Jumna. It contains what seem to have been two Dials, now in ruins. They are of brick of small dimensions, covered with a fine plaster or Chunam, and stand on the terrace of a good house.

9th March, *Chowmooa,* 12 m.—We passed through Muttra close to the Musjid,† a fine looking edifice covered with enamel, which must have had a splendid appearance when new. There is a pretty good Seraee at Chowmooa.

* Equal to £360,000.

† Musjid—mosque.

Last year on my road to this place, I deviated a little from the direct line, and visited Bindrabund, a spot famous in the history of Krishna. The morning was cool, the sky spotless, and the river, like a broad scarf of silver gauze fresh from the looms of Benares. It happened to be a day of jautra or pilgrimage, and the shores of the Jumna were crowded with devotees of both sexes, in all the various costumes of the East. The wealthy with their attendants in rich apparels, the Fakeers of the countless sects with their characteristic dresses, or rather undresses, and the women in flowing robes of different colours. In the distance at the Ghauts,* numbers of persons were performing their ablutions, throwing the water about in showers, which, lit by the beams of the rising sun, seemed as if they were scattering jewels. Along the banks were many elegant temples, and shady groves that very much increased the beauty of this scene of a Hindoo holiday.

Bindrabund (which signifies a grove of Toolsee

* Ghat, ferry, ford, pass, quay.

trees) is a considerable town surrounded by gardens, and groves. The streets are narrow, but well built, and the bazaars are abundantly supplied. There is only one very old temple in it, which contains the image of Govinda.* It is large and well designed, but has suffered greatly from the intolerance of the Mahummedans. The other temples are modern, and belong to persons of fortune, and rank. They are the most insignificant portion of the handsome houses to which they are attached. It is the fashion among Hindoo Rajahs, and other wealthy individuals, to have a residence at Bindrabund.†

* Govind is another name for Krishna.

† The following is taken from the 2nd vol. Transactions of the Royal Asiatic Society of Great Britain and Ireland, p. 99, and contains an account of everything worthy of notice from its sanctity at Bindrabund :—

" We then proceeded to Mathura, where having performed the religious ceremonies enjoined at the temples, we went to Vrindàvan (Binderabun). Here I bathed in the very pool where the divine Crishna crushed the serpent Kalya. We also saw the remains of the very Kadam-tree (Nauclea Orientalis) in which the god concealed himself after having stolen away the clothes of the shepherdesses who were bathing in the holy stream. At Binderabun we

10th March, *Dothanee,* 13 m.—On the road we passed through Chatta, a small town on rising ground, with a large Seraee of red stone, the gateways of which, crowned with pavilions, have a handsome appearance. Dothanee itself is a large village.

---

visited the several temples of Atal-behání, Kunj-behání, Banki-behání, Rádhá-Kishór, and Góvind-ji; all dedicated to the god Crishna in his various shapes. * * * I visited the tree of Rádhá (where Crishna assisted to dress his mistress), as also the wownsí-tree, under which he used to recline and play on his pipe. I likewise visited the Séva Ban and Kunj Ban, two groves where the god used to retire. The trees of the latter are rather low in stature; but they are very thickly studded with branches and leaves, affording a permanent shade. The grove abounds in trees of all kinds; but those whose nature it is to have thorns in other places, here have none. I was much delighted in these groves, and could fancy them still the retired abode of some divinity. I also went and rolled in the Ramal Reti (soft sand-hills in the bed of the Jumna) which still remain as in the time of the god.

One afternoon I paid a visit to the holy persons who reside at the spot called Dnyán Gújrí, with whom I was much pleased; and before dark I performed (Sandhya) prayers and ablutions at the Dhír Sumír, so called from the gentle and cool breezes which blow there in the evening across the waters of the Jumna."

11th March, *Puncharee,* 15 m.—We pitched our camp among fine trees near a tank. The village is small.

During the march we passed successively Kosee, Kotmun, and Hooraul. Kosee is a place of some commerce, in a fertile country amongst shady trees. Hooraul has been a considerable town, though it is now in a state of dilapidation. There are many large trees about it, and remains of Mahummedan buildings.

12th March, *Phulwal,* 15 m. 4 f.—The road run through an open jungle of bushes the whole way, although immediately about the villages the land was partially cultivated.

Bamineekera is a moderate village 9 m. 4 f. from our last encampment. We passed through it on the road.

From an Autobiographical Memoir of the early life of Nana Farnevis. Translated from the original Mahratta, by Lieut.-Colonel J. Briggs, M. R. A. S., late Resident at the Court of Satara. (Nana was born in 1742.)

There is also in this volume of the Researches an excellent paper by my late lamented friend Lieut.-Colonel James Tod, M. R. A. S., on the "Religious Establishments of Mewar," which details at length the history of Krishna.

Our tents were pitched close to a small gurhee just without the town of Phulwal, which once belonged to a Mahummedan chieftain. It has been a flourishing place, but the chieftain is dead, and it is falling fast into ruins.

13th March, *Ballumghur,* 13 m. 4 f.—For the first four or five miles, the road traversed the same kind of jungle as yesterday, and then became open, and cultivated. At 9 m. 4 f. from Phulwal we passed by Futteehpoor Sicri, a small village. It is a pleasant spot to encamp near. In the book of routes it is put down as 16 m. 4 f. from Bamineekera, but it appeared to us only 14 m. or 14 m. 4 f. from that place.

Ballumghur where we halted, is a small town, with a fort, in the possession of a Hindoo chief.

14th March, *Buddenpoor,* 11 m.—On our road we passed Furreedabad where there is a pretty musjid, which was erected by Jehaungeer. It is about 5 m. 4 f. from Ballumghur. At about the same distance further on is Kojaka-Seraee. The Seraee is spacious, but in ruins, as is also the town.

In the evening we rode towards Tooglichabad, and after passing it, reached some eminences near the Kootub minar, from whence we saw upon the arid, broken plain before us the ruins of Delhi.*

* All these buildings are modern, compared with those still to be seen at a place called Cootub Shah, seven computed coss to the S. W. of Dehli. This place is full of ruins and sepulchres; 180,000 saints and martyrs of the Islam, are computed to lie buried there, exclusive of Cootub O'din himself, who is one of their principal apostles. This spot is famous on account of the many battles which have been fought near it, by the first Mussulman conquerors against the Rajahs' of Dehli, the last of which, fought about 600 years ago against Rajah Paitowra, gave the decisive blow. * * * It appears to be 300 feet in height, and has been built with great care and niceness. Many verses of the Koran are carved on the stones in large characters; and the whole seems to have been intended as a lasting monument of the Islam, and to set forth its superiority to the Hindoo worship.—*Asiatic Annual Register*, 1799—*Misc. Tracts*, p. 39.

"No. 2 and 4 (Inscriptions on the Cootub Minar) are much to the same in purport, the latter a perfect fac-simile; and both state the Minar to have been built in the time of the Sultan Shems-ud-din Altemsh. * * *

"The above mentioned Sultan reigned from A.D. 1210 to 1231, corresponding with A. H. 607 and 629, and may be looked upon as the prince under whose auspices the Minar was completed.—*Asiatic Researches*, vol. 14, p. 481. Calcutta, Pereira, 1822.

The circumference of miles was strewed with the remains of this great city—the grave of splendour, the shattered, yet magnificent sepulchre of the Mighty! But the monuments that remain give an air of greater desolation to this scene, than all that the bloodstained arm of barbaric power, or the feverish hand of fanaticism could ever effect. We still see the massive bastions of Tooglichabad, the graceful tower of the Kootub, the marble domes, and minarets of the Jumma Musjid, the vast palace of Lal Killa, the old fort of Sherghur, and the sacred mausoleum of the good Hoomayoon.* Still they stand upon the earth, like a pallid crew upon a raft at the mercy of the unquiet, and boundless ocean, for what an ocean is time! These objects produce a multitude of reflections, but when we

* "The mildness and benevolence of Humaioon were excessive; if there can be any excess in virtues like these. His affection to his brothers proved the source of all his misfortunes; but (for?) they rewarded him with ingratitude and contempt. He was learned, a lover of literature, and the generous patron of the men of genius, who flourished in his time. In battle he was valiant and enterprizing; but the clemency of his disposition hindered him from using his

add to them the remembrance, that this capital of the once famed Moghul empire was but the offspring of one whose antiquity is lost in mystery, we become helpless, and gaze at vacancy.

Dehli was built upon the foundations of the ancient Indraput, the seat of the descendants of Pandoo, heroes of the Mahabarat.* Dehli was

---

victories in a manner which suited the vices of the times. Had he been less mild and religious, he would have been a more successful prince. Had he been a worse man he would have been a greater monarch."—*Dow's Hindostan*, vol. 2, p. 213.

* "Dehly is a very ancient city, which was formerly called Inderput."—*Ayeen Akbery*, vol. 2, p. 104.

"In the year 429 of the Æra of Bickermajeet, Anungpaul of the Tenore tribe governed with justice; and he founded the city of Dehly."—*Ayeen Akbery*, vol. 2, p. 118.

"Bickermajit flourished in the first century of the Christian æra, Note k."—*Maurice's Indian Antiquities*, Diss. 1, p. 48.

"With the aid of the priesthood and concurrence of the blind king Dhertrashtra, a partition of the dominion took place, when Yudishtra, the elder Pandu, was enthroned in Indraput, (*a*) which henceforth eclipsed the more ancient capital Hastinapoor."

(*a*) "Its name of Dehli is modern, having been given in the eighth century, by the Tuars, descended from the Pandus, who re-founded it."—*Lieut.-Colonel Tod's Compar.*

rebuilt, and received its present name in the reign of Anungpaul of the same race, but this was after the lapse of ages.* Dehli was conquered by Cootub ul deen Abiek, who although

---

of the Hindoo and Theban Hercules. Trans. R. A. S., vol. 3, pt. 1, p. 150.

"The first Indian poet was Valmici, author of the Ramayana, a complete Epick Poem on one continued, interesting, and heroick action; and the next in celebrity, if it be not superior in reputation for holiness, was the Mahabharata of Vyasa."—*Dissertations, &c., by Sir W. Jones and others*, vol. 2, p. 113. London, Nicol, 1792.

* "Cuttubeddin Ibec was the founder of the Patan or Afghan dynasty. He was a native of Afghanistan, or the country of the Afghans, and originally a slave. He was purchased by the late emperor, whose notice he soon attracted by his brilliant talents, and whose favour he gained by his ingenious disposition and firm fidelity."—*Asiatic Annual Register*, 1799, p. 22.

"He also drew his army towards Dehli and invested it. But the garrison finding that their own numbers triply exceeded the besiegers, marched out of the place, and drew up in order of battle, which was gladly accepted by Cuttub. When the slaughter became great on both sides, and the river Jumna was discoloured with blood, the Rajaputs were at length put to flight, taking protection within their walls. The garrison after a desperate siege, were at last obliged to capitulate." A. H. 588, A. D. 1192.—*Dow's Hindostan*, vol. 1, p. 153.

the slave of the Ghiznivide Emperor Mahummud Gori, became the founder of the Affghaun Dynasty in India. In less than two centuries after Tooglich erected a new city, which still bears his name, and its solid walls and towers attest the supremacy of their founder, and will proclaim his title through yet unseen vicissitudes.* But a more fearful desolation was to fall upon Dehli than any it had yet experienced. Timur assaulted it, and its ashes were its funeral pall, and crumbling palaces its chief mourners.† Nevertheless its form seemed endowed with immorta-

* "We have no true accounts of the Pedigree of Tuglick."

"When Tuglick mounted the throne, he began to regulate the affairs of government, which had fallen into the utmost disorder, by the most salutary and advisable methods, which gained him general esteem. He repaired the palaces and fortifications, founded others, &c."

"After the King's funeral obsequies were performed, his eldest son Jonah ascended the throne by the name of Mahommed, and proceeded from Tuglick Abad to Dehli." A.D. 1325.—*Dow's Hindostan*, vol. 1, p. 295 and 299.

† Timur invaded India in 1397; and upon arriving before Dehli he had upwards of 100,000 prisoners. On their showing some joy at seeing him attacked, whilst reconnoitering the place, he ordered all above the age of 15 to be massa-

lity, for in a few generations it again asserted its pre-eminence, and upon the defeat of Ibrahim Lodi in 1525 by the Sultaun Baber it became the regal city of the Moghul empire.* Hoomayoon ruled here, was driven from here, but returned victorious, died, and was buried here.† His son

---

cred. One hundred thousand were killed on this command. Mahmood III., the reigning Emperor, engaged with Timur before the gates of Dehli, but was routed with great slaughter, and took refuge in the town, from whence he and his minister, fearing to be seized by the victor, fled. Timur then received the submission of the Omrahs and great men, and soon after ordered himself to be proclaimed in the city. However, much trouble was given by the contributions which he had levied upon entering Dehli not being paid. A confusion took place, force was employed, and—

"The Hindoos, according to their manner, seeing their wives and daughters ravished and polluted, * * shut the city gates, set fire to their houses, murthered their wives and children, and ran out like madmen against their enemies."

"But little effect had the despair of the unfortunate upon the Moguls, who soon collected themselves, and began a general massacre. Some streets were rendered impassable by the heaps of dead: and in the mean time the gates being forced, the whole Mogul army were admitted. Then followed a scene of horror much easier to be imagined than described."—*Dow's Hindostan*, vol. 2, p. 5, et seq.

* Vide Paneeput, p. 47.

† See note, ante p. 30.

Ackbar the Great raised a superb mausoleum over the remains of his father, but forsook the city, and founded Agra.* During the reign of his son Jehaungeer, nothing of any great merit was added to Dehli, but its fame was increased; for the Empress of Jehaungeer was the lovely and talented Noormahal.† Shauh Jehaun succeeded, and perceiving Dehli decline, for during the last

* See note, ante p. 20.

† "The extraordinary beauty of her person has been already mentioned; we shall now delineate the features of her mind. Her abilities were uncommon; for she rendered herself absolute, in a government in which women are thought incapable of bearing any part. Their power, it is true, is sometimes exerted in the haram; but like the virtues of the magnet, it is silent and unperceived. Noor Jehan stood forth in public; she broke through all restraint and custom, and acquired power by her own address, more than by the weakness of Jehangire. Ambitious, passionate, insinuating, cunning, bold and vindictive, yet her character was not stained with cruelty; and she maintained the reputation of chastity when no restraint but virtue remained. Her passions were indeed too masculine. When we see her acting the part of a soldier, she excites ridicule more than admiration; and we are apt to forget that delicacy beyond which her sex ceases to please."

Her original name was Mher-ul-Nissa—then Noormahal and Noorjehan. She died at Lahore, in 1645.—*Dow's Hindostan*, vol. 3, p. 184.

reign the court had been at Agra, he reared it anew from the dust, and called it after his own name Shauhjehaunabad.* The Jumma Musjid arose, the Palace of Lal Killa was erected and furnished with all that was costly, the ceiling of its Dewan Khass was covered with plates of pure gold; and in the midst the peacock throne blazed with the light of the most precious gems in oriental gorgeousness. Ali Murdaun Khaun, one of his Omrahs, conducted a canal, more than a hundred miles in length, from the Jumna at Moghulpoor, near Kurnaul, to the principal streets of the imperial city, a work as beneficent as it was princely;† and the Royal Gardens of Shalimar bloomed.‡ In one century more Nadir Shauh entered Dehli as a conqueror, and upon some

* "Actuated partly by these motives, and partly by the desire of immortalizing his name, in the erection of a city that should exceed in grandeur all the other cities of Hindostan, Jehaun Shaw, the grandson of Acbar, in A.D. 1647, according to Fraser, rebuilt Dehli from the ground, and called the new city Jehaunabad, after his own name."—*Maurice's Indian Antiquities*, Diss. I., page 58, et seq.

† Vide Kurnaul, p. 50.

‡ Vide Alipoor, p. 41.

reprisal made on his licentious soldiery, he ordered a general massacre of its inhabitants, and levelled their dwellings. Now pillage upon pillage was its doom. One of its Emperors was assassinated and two were inhumanly blinded; its almost defenceless people were slaughtered, and their decaying habitations ransacked; till at length the Redcross banner of St. George floated from the ramparts of its citadel, and the Emperor, though the faintest shadow of a shadow, lived in security, and must I add, still in pride.*

* "Ahmed Shah was, soon afterwards, deprived of his throne and sight, at Dehli, by Akbut Mahmood Khan, Gazy O'Deen Khan's tutor; and from that period may be dated the total ruin and subversion of the empire, and of this city in particular. The enmity that subsisted among the great Omrahs, and the late doings of Gazy, obliged him (Akbut Mahmood Khan) for his own safety, to maintain a large body of mercenary Mahrattas, and Rohillas; * * * The Rohillas in particular * * . They alone were the principal cause of the destruction of this once opulent and splendid city. The devastations and plunders of Nadir Shah, and Ahmed Shah Abdallah were like violent tempests, which, for the time, carried every thing before them, but soon subsided; whereas the waste and havoc made by the Rohillas resembled pestilential gales, which keep up a continual agitation, and finally destroy a country. Certain it is,

Such has been the fate of this eastern capital. If all the treasure which has been lavished here were amassed, it would form a pyramid of gold. If all the blood which has been shed here could gush again from the earth, it would cover to the house tops. If the bones of its unsepulchred

---

their very name is in detestation in this place."—*Extracts from Letters from Major Polier at Dehli to Col. Ironside, at Belgram, May 22nd, 1776. Asiatic Ann. Register*, 1800. *Misc. Tracts*, p. 40, et seq.

" Nadir Shah entered Dehli on the 9th March, 1739.

" Ahmed Shah blinded and dethroned, 1735.

" Alumgeer assassinated in 1756, in which year Ahmed Shah Abdalli first entered Dehli.

" Shah Jehan the Second dethroned, in 1760.

" In 1788, Gholaum Kaudir, the Rohilla, having, by a sudden irruption, made himself master of Dehli, seized the unfortunate Emperor (Shah Allum), and after exposing him for many weeks to every species of insult and degredation, in order to extort the disclosure of supposed concealed treasures, concluded by piercing his eyes with a dagger so as completely to extinguish the sight."—*Hamilton's Account of Hindostan.* Dehli.

" The visit of the Commander in Chief to his Majesty was fixed at eight this morning, &c. * * *
The prospect of a handsome nuzzur or offering operated with the King to facilitate the presentation; for it is known that by such means he is necessitated to eke out the scanty pittance allowed to him and his numerous family, servants,

throngs were heaped up, instead of a level plain we should see a mountain. If all the silent thoughts of its aggrieved poor could rush into voice, that voice would strike oppression dead, and proclaim to the world "Beware of tyranny, yet in the strength of freedom tyrannize not." Dehli has been the stage of greatness, Men the actors, Ambition the prompter, Centuries the audience.

---

and dependants residing in the fort."—*Archer's Tours in Upper India*, vol. 1, p. 110, et seq.

For the sake of contrast, the following note is subjoined.—Editor.

"The first English ship which came to Surat was the Hector, commanded by Captain William Hawkins, who brought a letter from the Company, and another from the King, James I., to the great Mogul Jehangire, requesting the intercourse of trade.

"The Hector arrived at Surat in August, 1608; but as in a voyage of experiment, * * *

"Fortunately at this time news came to Agra of the arrival of Sir Henry Middleton at Surat, when Hawkins formally demanded his dismission from the Mogul, and requested an answer to the letter he had brought from the King, which was denied; but he was permitted to depart, and arrived at Cambay on the 11th December, 1611."—*Orme's Historical Fragments*, p. 319, et seq. London. Wingrave, 1805, 4to.

Destruction has drawn the curtain, and the moral is: "Which of you by taking thought can add one cubit unto his stature."*

15th March, *Dehli,* 12 m.—Upon leaving Buddenpoor we rode to Hoomayoon's Tomb, Munsur Ali's Durga, and the Jumtra Muntra or Jey Singhs Observatory, from whence we proceeded to the modern town where we encamped.

In the evening we went to see the shawl manufactory (which is the only one out of Cashmere) and were much pleased with it. There are seven looms, which are worked by natives of Cashmere, from whence the shawl wool thread which is required also comes. The number of bobbins used at once are between 1500 and 2000, and a shawl of large size requires six or eight months in making.

Halted 16th March.

17th March, *Alipoor,* 12 m.—This is a small village in an agreeable plain. We visited the celebrated gardens of Shalimar, upon which Shauh

* Matth., c. vi., v. 27.

Jehaun is reported to have spent one million sterling.[*] They are about two miles and a half in circumference; and all that remains of their former beauty are a few insignificant buildings, and the brick wall which surrounded them. Sir David Ochterlony has erected a handsome house here, and bestowed some care upon the grounds.

To-day is the festival of the Hoolee,[†] and our camp is a scene of unbounded rejoicing. The

* Hamilton's Account of Hindoostan. Dehli.

† "During the Huli, when mirth and festivity reign among Hindus of every class, one subject of diversion is to send people on errands and expeditions that are to end in disappointment, and raise a laugh at the expense of the person sent. The Huli is always in March, and the last day is the greatest holiday. * *

"The origin of the Huli seems lost in antiquity; and I have not been able to pick up the smallest account of it, * * * may not the custom of making April fools, on the first of that month, indicate some traces of the Huli? * * * with us it is chiefly confined to the lower classes of people; but in India high and low join in it; and the late Shujaul Daulah, I am told, was very fond of making Huli fools, though he was a Muselman of the highest rank."—*Dissertations and Miscellaneous Pieces*, by Sir W. Jones and others. The extract is from one by Colonel Pearse, May 12th, 1785, vol. 2, p. 194, et seq. London, Nicol, &c. 1792, 2 vols., 8vo.

servants, and other followers, both Hindoos and Mahummedans, are strolling about in groups, accompanied with the clashing of rude music, to which they add yells of merriment, and songs especially chanted upon this holiday. They are provided with quantities of a red powder, which they throw at each other, and besides, mix it with water, and squirt the concoction, with extreme ingenuity, by means of monster syringes, at all comers. Here we see a crowd of young urchins, their eyes on fire with innocent subtlety, splashing a venerable Mahummedan, whose long beard soon reeks with the crimson streams of the Hoolee water, while, he in return, shaking with laughter, envelops them suddenly in a cloud of the rosy powder.

"In the month of Phagum. The eleventh Tit'h of Suckulputch, which they call Hoolee. * * It is a season of great merriment, which is much increased by throwing at one another powders of different colours. On the last night they light fires, and throw into them various things. This is a Sooder festival. The twenty-ninth day and night of this month they call Sewrat. They keep awake all night, and account it lucky for particular undertakings."—*Ayeen Akbery*, vol. 3, p. 270.

"Hoolee! Hoolee!" is the cry. There you see a neat and staid Khidmutgar,* his white dress dyed with a hue like the rich red beams of day-break, leaping with frenzied mirth to the eloquent melody of tom-toms,† regardless of tent-ropes, and tent-pins, in the midst of a throng of coolies,‡ smiling at all, and enchanted with himself; now he disappears in whirlwinds of ruby dust, now he rises beneath rainbows of blushing waterdrops, which career arching over his head. Sometimes he pursues, sometimes he runs away, while shrieks of ecstacy are heard. "Hoolee! Hoolee! Hoolee! Hoolee!" Here we have a muscular Seapoy vociferating, and twirling like a dancing Durwesh,§ an excited statute of red-granite; and look you at that laughing Hindoostanee girl, whose supple figure moves as gracefully as a

* Khidmutgar, attendant, butler, servant.

† Drums.

‡ Koolee, goolee, porter, carrier.

§ "The Mewlewi Derwishes: sort of Turkish friars, whose devout exercises consist in twirling round like tops." —*Hope's Anastasius*, vol. i. chap. vii. note 9.

Lotos stem,* in an imperceptible eddy, whose large black eyes are liquid with excess of delight, her thin white garment spotted and streaked with the carmine water, bending her neck, and putting her little hand into a large bag, and taking out as much of the glowing powder, as it will hold—

* Nelumbium speciosum. De Cand. Reg. Veg. Syst. Nat. vol. ii. p. 44, et seq. " Flores pulcherrimi," (albi aut rosœi). Nunc in Indiâ et Chinâ australi frequens et inter plantas sacras diù habita, (and above) Petioli longi, teretes, erecti, extra aquam exserti, *tuberculis acutis subretrorsis scabri.* The true Lotos is called by De Candolle " Nymphœa Lotus," and does not grow in India, vide p. 52, of the work above quoted. The Lotos so frequently mentioned in all translations from the Sanscrit, it is presumed therefore, is the " Nelumbium speciosum."

" The reservoir glows with the red lotus blossoms, like the dawn with the fiery beams of the rising sun."—*Wilson's Hindu Theatre,* vol. i. p. 88. London. Parbury, 1835.

" May her way be attended with prosperity! May propitious breezes sprinkle, for her delight, the odoriferous dust of rich blossoms! May pools of clear water, green with the leaves of the Lotos, refresh her as she walks! and may shady branches be her defence from the scorching sun-beams."—*Sacontala,* p. 89. Cooper. Calcutta, 1789.

Calidasa, the author of Sacontala, was a close observer of nature, as may be judged by the following passage, and it also goes far to prove that the Water Lily, or as it is also called the Lotos, was the Nelumb. spec. just mentioned. e. g.

"Hoolee! Hoolee! Hoolee! Hoolee!" All is uproar, all is confusion, all is pleasure!

The merry-making was continued during the greater part of the night, and the next morning when we started, our cavalcade had a most ludicrous appearance.

18th March, *Soneeput.* Fifteen miles to the centre of the town, which being built on high ground has a striking appearance from a distance. It is however in a sad state of decay, and its ruins cover an extensive space. On the Dehli side there is a large Seraee, in tolerable preservation. On the road we passed by Nureela, a good sized town on an elevated spot, in the midst of ruins where there is a magnificent tank, built of brick, but it is now dry, and its area cultivated. Nureela is

---

" Many are the *rough stalks* which support the water-lily; but many and exquisite are the blossoms, which hang on them."—*Sacontala*, p. 14.

De Candolle's description of the Nelumb. spec.

" Penduncuili teretes, petiolis longiores, erecti, *scabri.*" vide supra.

Calidasa flourished in the first century, B. C. in the reign of Vicramaditya.

4m. 4f. from our last encampment. At about the same distance onwards, we came to the Baroutee Seraee, a spacious building, pleasantly situated.

Just after we had quitted our tents this morning, the range of mountains above Hurdwar became visible on our right, and continued so until sunrise.

Thermometer at daybreak, 54° Fahrenheit; between 2 and 3 P. M. 84°.

19th March, *Gônore*, 7m. 4f. A small village with an old Seraee. Before sunrise we had a fine view of the Hurdwar hills, distant in a direct line more than 110 miles. It seemed as if we could have reached them at a smart canter in six hours. The country is pretty, and tolerably well cultivated.

Thermometer at daybreak, 57° Fahrenheit; in the afternoon, 88°.

20th March. *Somalka,* 6 miles. There is some mistake in the route book, as we make Somalka from Soneeput, only 13m. 4f. which seems correct. We marched to-day through a pleasant though not highly cultivated country, and again saw the range above Hurdwar. Somalka is a moderate sized village, with a large ruinous Seraee. The fields are now watered by means of the Persian Wheel.

21st March, *Paneeput*, 10m. 4f. About 1m. 4f. we passed Kurris, a large village with tanks near it at the entrance of the low jungle, which extended to within five miles of this place. The Hurdwar hills were visible during the march.

Paneeput is a considerable town, built of brick, and seated on some rising ground in the midst of a very extensive plain. It was upon this plain that two battles were fought, which decided the fate of two of the greatest powers in India. The first was in 1525, between the small army of the Sultaun Baber, and the vast force of the Patan Emperor of Dehli Ibrahim Lodi, in which the latter was killed, and his army defeated and dispersed; the Patan dynasty overthrown and the Moghul established.* The second was in 1761,

* "The imperial army under Ibrahim, by this time consisted of one hundred thousand horse, and a thousand elephants; that of Baber, of thirteen thousand only;" p. 117.

between the Mahommedan force under the command of Ahmed Shauh Abdaullee, of Candahar, and the Mahrattas, under Bhaw Sidasiva.* This contest almost annihilated the Mahrattas, who, had they been victorious, would have seized the Punjaub, and bounded their territory only by the Indus.

A venerable old Moosoolmaun, eighty-two years of age, who had been an eye witness of this murderous conflict, came to our tents and gave us an account of it. The principal features of his narrative were the same as those inserted in the Asiatic Researches, which is a translation from a

---

" According to the most moderate accounts, there were sixteen thousand Patans killed in this action, though most authors say fifty thousand. Of the loss of Baber we have no information: conquerors having it always in their power to conceal the number of their slain. We may date from this battle the fall of the Patan empire, though that race afterwards made many efforts, and recovered it for a few years. as we shall see in the life of Humaioon."—*Dow's Hind ostan*, v. 2. p. 119.

* For an account of Ahmed Shauh Ahdaullee, see Hon. M. Elphinstone's Caubul; vol. ii. appendix A, p. 279.

Ahmed Shauh Abdaullee invaded India six times.—*Maurice's Indian Ant. Diss.* i. p. 61

detailed memoir, also by an eye witness. How quiet is the plain now!

Paneeput is fast verging to ruin. There is a shrine here which is held in much sanctity, said to be that of a Mahummedan saint, named Shereef ud Deen Abu Ali Callinder, a descendant of the prophet, as his title of "Shereef" indicates.

Thermometer at day-break, 62° Fahrenheit; in the afternoon, 93°.

22nd March, *Gorounda,* 9m. 4f.—We traversed a pleasant country, partially under tillage, and pitched our tents here, on a fine level piece of ground, near a handsome Seraee of red-stone. The morning was cloudy, and we therefore did not see the Hurdwar mountains.

Last night five Nautch women sung and danced in our tents for a couple of hours. They were dressed in dark purple Dhoputtahs, broadly edged with silver. Neither the singing nor the dancing was good, with the exception of the Khurwa Nautch, which was excellent. One of the party, a young girl of 13 or 14, who was very pretty, and one of the women, danced it.

23rd March, *Kurnaul*, 11m.—Our route was through a jungle, which extended to the bridge over Ali Murdaun Khaun's canal,* which is within about four miles of the British cantonments.

We halted here during the 24th to prepare for

* "But what gave the greatest lustre and splendour to the new city, was the successful attempt of Ally Murdaun Khan, a Persian Omrah (the same who delivered Candahar into Shah Jehan's hands), who undertook to bring a canal of fresh water, to run through the principal streets and parts of the town, by a cut made from the Jumna itself, at a place called Mogulpoor (about 60 coss from Dehli), where the river is very rapid, and has several falls; and this, by a proper management, he soon effected. Though the work was not done with that elegance and solidity for which the ancient, and some of our modern aqueducts are so famous, yet it was not the less useful; and it may easily be conceived what pleasure in such a climate as this, and in a place too where there is not a potable well, the sight of a canal of excellent water must afford, running through every principal street in the town, and through the gardens and houses of the Omrahs and chief inhabitants. The work was mostly done with earth, and therefore required constant attendance and repair; but the advantage of having such an immense body of water at command, through so long a course as nearly 120 miles of country, amply compensated every expense."—*Asiatic Annual Register*, *Misc. Tracts*, p. 37, 1800.

It went to ruin, was again repaired, by Ahmed Shah Duranny (Abdaullee); but during the Mahratta troubles was again dried up. It is now once more opened.

our future progress, and therefore provided ourselves with smaller trunks to contain our baggage, and a variety of other things, which we supposed would be useful during our tour in the Himala.

Kurnaul is a military station of importance from its position, as it is upon the very verge of the confederate Sikh states, under the protection of the British Government, as well as from its forming a support to our advanced post at Loodeanah, and covering both Dehli, and the Dooaub in our rear, from any sudden irruption from the districts of the Punjaub. Its climate is healthy, the surrounding country open, and water abundant.

Our journey now becomes interesting from other circumstances than those which have lately commanded our attention. We are about to leave the perishing records of man, for the imperishable records of nature. To-morrow also we shall be among the Sikhs, and shall be able, though superficially, to judge of the effects, which the subversion of the sacred Hindoo law of Casts,* produces

* Nanac Shah, founder of the Sect since distinguished by the name of Sikh's, was born in the year of Christ 1469, at

upon men, whose forefathers had so religiously obeyed its injunctions, for more than two thousand five hundred years; supposing we date its origin, only from the time of Menu, which is the smallest period we may reasonably assign. But it is the Himalaya, the sublime, the sacred Himalaya, which is the perpetual discourse of our imaginations. From the first correct accounts I had perused of these giant mountains, I had longed ardently to see them, to be upon them, to know them. The very impulse brought back to me my school days

---

a small village called Talwandi, in the district of Bhatti, in the province of Lahore.

Talwandi is now called Rayapur. It is situated on the banks of the Beyah, or Hyphasis.

"The object of Nanac was to abolish the distinction of cast amongst the Hindus, and to bring them to the adoration of that Supreme Being, before whom all men, he contended, were equal. Guru Govind, who adopted all the principles of his celebrated predecessor, as far as religious usages were concerned, is reported to have said, on this subject, that the four tribes of Hindus, the Brahmen, Cshatriya, Vaisya, and Sudra, would, like pan, (betle leaf), chunam, (lime), supari, (betle-nut), and khat, (terra japonica or catechu), become all of one colour when well chewed."—*Sir J. Malcolm's Sketch of the Sikhs.* Note, p. 45.

among the purple hills of the Vale of Clwyd, and the freshness of the summer mornings, so different from the Deccan, where, in the hot weather, though the Acacia intensely perfumed the air, there was not a blade of grass to betoken coolness. And am I so near the accomplishment of my desires!

CHAPTER II.

KURNAUL TO SUBAHTOO.

25th March, *Azimabad*, 8m.—On quitting the Parade at Kurnaul we entered a jungle abounding with black partridge, which continued about five miles and a half to the village of Shamghur. The country then became partially cultivated.

Shamghur belongs to the Sikhs, but we only saw two or three of this sect, the villagers being principally Jauts and Moosoolmauns.

We had a delightful view of the Hurdwar range in the morning.

The town of Azimabad is upon some rising ground, and is surrounded with a brick wall. There is a handsome tank here with flights of steps leading down to the water, built of brick; and a very large Seraee in good repair.

Thermometer at day-break, 55° Fahrenheit; in the afternoon, 88°.

26th March, *Tanasur,* 14m. 2f.—The road was rather uneven for the three miles between Neelokeree and Azimabad, and was also intersected by the Chittung nullah. In the rainy season this part of the country is very swampy, and from its clayey nature difficult for the passage of artillery. After leaving Neelokeree, and another village called Raeepoor, we traversed a jungle of Dawk* and Baubool† trees, and came to Sumoonah, which is six miles distant from Tanasur. The villages were very wretched looking places, with usually a small number of brick buildings. We saw but few Sikhs.

Along the first half of our march the land was tilled and fertile: indeed the soil is equal to that south of Kurnaul, and is as plentifully supplied with water; men and cattle are alone wanting to make it fully productive of all kinds of grain.

* Butea frondosa. De Candolle. Prod. v. 2, spec. 1, p. 415. Dhak or Dawk.

† Acacia arabica. De Candolle. Prod. v. 2, spec. 135, p. 461. Baubool.

During the whole day we have been admiring the Choor Pahar, one of the high mountains of the lower Himala, the summit of which is covered with snow, a novelty we have not seen for many years; and though the duties of a soldier's life have given somewhat of sternness to the character, still we longed, like children, to pelt each other with hard snow balls. When we arrived at Tanasur, we had our tents pitched to the north of the town upon a green turf shaded by lofty trees. It was a delightful spot, and the tanks, mausoleums, and ruins, formed a beautiful picture before us.

Tanasur* is one of the most celebrated places in India. It was formerly filled with temples whose imposing forms were only surpassed by the costliness of their sanctuaries. Pilgrims crowded to Tanasur. The venerated stream, the Surris-

* "Tahnesir is held sacred by the Hindoos. The river Sirsutty, to which they pay profound adoration, runs near it; and in its vicinity is the venerated lake Koorket. This was the scene of the Mahabbarut, or the great war."—*Maurice's Indian Antiquities*, Diss. 1, p. 133.

wutty, flowed past it.* In the neighbourhood were the Plains of Koorket, so famed in the sacred stanzas of the Mahabarat. It was the capital of a powerful kingdom, it was the fane of deified heroes, the seat of Hierophants of many mysteries. What could more attract crowds of human beings to Tanasur than these objects?

After sun-set, when the air was cool, we rode out; and as the principal subject of our curiosity

* "The confluence of the Ganga and Yamuna (Jumna) at Prayaga, is called Triveni by the Pauranics, because three rivers are supposed to meet there; but the third is by no means obvious to the sight. It is the famous Sarasvati, which comes out of the hills to the west of the Yamuna, passes close to Thaneser, loses itself in the great sandy desert, and re-appears at Prayag, humbly oozing from under one of the towers of the fort, as if ashamed of herself. Indeed she may blush at her own imprudence; for she is the goddess of learning and knowledge, and was then coming down the country with a book in her hand, when she entered the sandy desert, and unexpectedly was assailed by numerous demons, with frightful countenances, making a dreadful noise. Ashamed at her own want of foresight, she sank into the ground, and re-appeared at Prayaga or Allahabad, for, as justly observed, learning is alone insufficient."—*On the Ancient Geography of India*, by Lieut.-Colonel Wilford. Trans. As. Soc., v. 14, p. 395.

was the lake Koorket, or Pandookund, we did not enter the mausoleum of Sheikh Chillee, a handsome edifice, with a dome of white marble, enclosed in a large fortified court-yard, but passed it, and proceeded at once to the Pandookund. As well as I can judge, it is about one mile in length, and half a mile in width. In the centre is an island 235 paces in breadth, connected with the shore on each side by two ancient bridges, 235 paces in length each, which, I was informed, are during the rainy season, covered with the water of the flooded lake. There is a third bridge also which leads to the island, said to have been built by Aurungzeeb, but it is now useless and broken. There are no temples here; but at the most hallowed spots flights of steps run down to the water's edge, for the convenience of those desirous of performing the usual ablutions.

It was upon the plains near this spot that the contending armies of the Kooroos and Pandoos fought. Of this conflict history has almost forgotten the date; but poetry has detailed every incident which attended it, with circumstance and reality. The simple tale is nearly as follows.*

Vichitra, King of Hastinapoor, had three daughters, two of whom became the mothers of the heroes of this war. Ambca the elder gave birth to Dhreetarashtra; Ambalica the younger, sur-

* "The Mahabharat contains the genealogy and general history of the house of Bhaurut, so called from Bhurrut, its founder; the epithet Maha or Great, being prefixed in token of distinction: but its more particular object is to relate the dissensions and wars of the two great collateral branches of it, called Kooroos and Pandoos; both lineally descended in the second degree from Veecheetrâveerya, their common ancestor, by their respective fathers Dreetrarashtra and Pandoo."—P. 6.

"This book (Mahabharat) is said to consist of more than one hundred thousand metrical stanzas." P. 11.—*Wilkin's Bhagvat-Geeta.* London. Nourse, 1785, 1 vol., 4to.

Vide also *Ayeen Akbery*, vol. 2, p. 107, et seq., where the details are given.

According to a paper by the late Lieut.-Col. Tod, on the Hindu and Theban Hercules (Trans. R. Asiatic Society, vol. 3, part 1, page 148), Vichitra reigned between the eleventh and twelfth centuries A.C. In the note, page 147, 'Vyasu, author or compiler of the Vedas, was the son of King Santana by Yojnaganda;' and, on the top of the page, 'Vyasu, their Guru, or spiritual father, the sole male of the house of Santana, took his niece, his spiritual daughter Pandea, to wife. She bore him Pandu, who succeeded to the

named Pandea, to Pandoo. Upon the death of Vichitra, the kingdom devolved on the elder born Dhreetarashtra; but as he was blind, his brother Pandoo governed in his stead. Dhreetarashtra, who was also named Kooroo, from a celebrated ancestor, had many sons, the eldest of whom was Dooryodhan. Pandoo had five sons, whose virtues and noble conduct have immortalized them with the title of the "Five Pandoos." They were respectively called Yoodeeshteer, Bheem, Arjoon, Nakool, and Sahadeva. When their father Pandoo died, their cousin Dooryodhan, jealous of the affection in which they were held by the people, fomented discords and factions, and at length expelled them from Hastinapoor, and assumed the conduct of the State. Various were

---

sovereignty of Northern India, and which, from that time, has been designated the Panduan Raj, or Kingdom of the Pandus. It is generally acknowledged that Vyasu or Vyasa was the author of the Mahabarat. Vide note, p. 32 ante. The orthography of the names differs in all three of the works consulted, viz. the Ayeen Akbery, Tod's Paper, and the Bhagvat Geeta; but that of the latter has been followed.

the fortunes of the Pandoos during their exile. After several years, however, they returned to the capital of their forefathers and obtained justice. A partition of the empire was effected; and while Dooryodhan retained Hastinapoor, Yoodeeshteer the eldest Pandoo was crowned King of Indraput, or, as it is now called, Dehli. Still Dooryodhan was of too evil a disposition to remain long satisfied, even with justice, and he again drove the Pandoos into banishment. But virtue, like the tender jessamine, the further it is forced to stray by obstacles, the more blossoms it bears, the more perfume it gives; so was it with the Pandoos: their misfortunes became a blessing to many, and even children uttered their praises, and sought, like them, to do good. Once more they returned to Hastinapoor, when Dooryodhan offered them battle upon the plains of Koorket, and summoned his army, which was so formidable, that nothing but the firmness of morality could have confronted it fearlessly. A host of thousands came upon war elephants, another multitude were in armed chariots, and many were the agitated throngs of horsemen, and the dense crowds of foot soldiers. The army of the Pandoos, led by their brother Bheem, was inconsiderable; but they came resolved for victory. How widely the combatants stretch along the plain, arrayed in all the bewitching glory of war, proud in the force of manhood, proud in the assurance of defending their honor and their right. They draw near. Upon the small space between them depends the possession of a kingdom and Peace, peace whose flowing garments of white are embroidered with blood!

"At this time Kreeshna and Arjoon were standing in a splendid chariot drawn by white horses."

"Arjoon, perceiving that the sons of Dhreetarashtra stood ready to begin the fight, and that the weapons began to fly abroad, having taken up his bow, addressed Kreeshna in the following words:

"I pray thee, Kreeshna, cause my chariot to be driven and placed between the two armies, that I may behold who are the men that stand ready, anxious to commence the bloody fight; and with whom it is that I am to fight in this ready field;

and who they are that are here assembled to support the vindictive son of Dhreetarashtra in the battle."

"Kreeshna being thus addressed by Arjoon, drove the chariot; and having caused it to halt in the midst of the space in front of the two armies, Arjoon cast his eyes towards the ranks of the Kooroos, and beheld where stood the aged Bheeshma, and Dron, with all the chief nobles of their party. He looked at both the armies, and beheld, on either side, none but grandsires, uncles, cousins, tutors, sons, and brothers, near relations, or bosom friends; and when he had gazed for a while, and beheld such friends as these prepared for the fight, he was seized with extreme pity and compunction, and uttered his sorrow in the following words:

"Having beheld, O Kreeshna! my kindred thus standing anxious for the fight, my members fail me, my countenance withereth, my hair standeth on end upon my body, and all my frame trembleth with horror! Even Gandeev, my bow, escapeth from my hand, and my skin is parched and dried up. I am not able to stand; for my comprehension, as it were, turneth round, and I behold inauspicious omens on all sides. When I shall have destroyed my kindred, shall I longer look for happiness? I wish not for victory, Kreeshna; I want not dominion; I want not pleasure; for what is dominion, and the enjoyments of life, or even life itself, when those, for whom dominion, pleasure, and enjoyment were to be coveted, have abandoned life and fortune, and stand here in the field ready for the battle? Tutors, sons and fathers, grandsires and grandsons, uncles and nephews, cousins, kindred, and friends! Although they would kill me, I wish not to fight them; no, not even for the dominion of the three regions of the universe, much less for this little earth!"*

* To give some idea of the beauty of Hindoo Literature to the generality, who have little leisure to examine such a subject, the Editor has taken the liberty of extracting this portion of the Bhagvat Geeta, or Dialogues of Kreeshna and Arjoon, which is an episode in the Mahabarat, a poem which the celebrated Hastings said, was 'worked up with wonderful fertility of genius and pomp of language into a

But the combat begins. Already the shock of the elephants is felt, and their subdued cries heard. The warriors are hand to hand, chest to chest; their breath inflamed and heated, burns their flushed cheeks in the close-locked struggles; the edge of battle begins to totter, and then suddenly the huge wave of living warriors rolls heavily over the bloody heaps of the dead and dying, and breaks in horrible destruction. The shattered ranks of the Kooroos still resist desperately, and fearful is the slaughter. The names of twelve only are recorded in the immortal pages of the Mahabarat as having survived this sanguinary conflict. Four were of the army of Dooryodhan, and eight of the

---

thousand sublime descriptions;' and, again, 'With the deductions, or rather qualifications, which I have thus premised, I hesitate not to pronounce the Geeta a performance of great originality; of a sublimity of conception, reasoning, and diction, almost unequalled; and a single exception among all the known religions of mankind, of a theology accurately corresponding with that of the Christian dispensation, and most powerfully illustrating its fundamental doctrines."—See *Warren Hastings' Letter to Nathaniel Smith, Esq.*, prefixed to Wilkins' Translation of the Bhagvat Geeta, p. 11.

Pandoo army, including the "Five Brothers." This poem further informs us, that after this event, Yoodeeshteer reigned prosperously for many years, and then forsaking the cares of the throne and tiara, he retired with his brethren into solitude.

Tanasur was also one of the number of those unfortunate cities which were doomed to defilement, plunder, and ruin, by the founder of the Ghiznivide race, the ruthless Mahmood. It was in 1011, A. D. that, regardless of the immense offers of ransom from his ally, Annindpal, and other Hindoo Rajahs, he assaulted this holy place, with his barbarian troops, beneath the green banners of the Prophet, and committed all the desperate violence which fanaticism, incited by the lust for gold, revels in.*

Thermometer at day-break, 58° Fahrenheit; in the afternoon, 89°.

27th March, *Keiree*, 14m.—Quitting our camp, and immediately crossing the sacred Surriswutty, we left the royal road from Agra to Lahore,† and

* Dow's History of Hindostan, vol. 1, p. 51, et seq.

† "Lastly, to make you pass quickly those fifty and sixty leagues which are betwixt Dehli and Agra, you are not to

proceeded by a very rough one to this place, which is a small village, pleasantly situated.

We passed in succession Dooraulla, 3m. 4f.; Saulpoonee, 2m. 4f.; Gaujpoor and the Maurkoonda nullah, 2m.; from whence it was six miles to Keiree. The country on this side Saulpoonee was well wooded and highly cultivated. It rained during our march.

28th March, *Nunoola*, 12m.—This is a considerable village in a charming country, but it is much decayed, as are most of the places in these parts, in consequence of the revolutions of the petty states. The road to-day was very bad;

---

think, that upon this road you shall see any such large and rich burroughs as there are upon our roads. Set aside Maturas, where you see still an ancient and stately Temple of Idols, and excepting some Karavan-sarrahs, that are well enough, found on the high-way to serve for night-lodgings, I find nothing considerable there, but that Royal Alley of Trees planted by command of Jehan-Guire; and continued by the same order for an hundred and fifty leagues, with little pyramids or turrets erected every half league, to mark the ways, and with frequent wells to afford drink to passengers, and to water the young trees."—*Bernier's Letter to M. de la Mothe le Vayer*, containing the description of Dehli and Agra.

indeed almost unfit for our baggage carts: in the rains it would be nearly impassable. We passed by Soonta on the Omrah nuddee, 4m.; Bhoonee, 2m. 4f.; Jaulbaira, 2m.; Towra, 4m.; and on to Nunoola, which was three miles further. The country was, as usual, perfectly level; and between Soonta and Towra covered with grass jungle. Heavy dews fall in this district. The morning was extremely sharp and fresh.

Thermometer at day-break, 56° Fahrenheit; in the afternoon, 87°.

29th March, *Putteeala,* 12m. — We passed through Punkhur, and Sanowree, the latter a small town eight miles from Nunoola. Also crossed two nullahs; the one about a mile from Punkhur we had considerable difficulty in fording; the other called the Kosilla, is a small branch of the Caggar river, and is close to Putteeala. The road was bad, but the country was very fertile.

The town of Putteeala is compact built chiefly of brick, and is thickly inhabited. The Rajah's residence is in a small, but not strong citadel.

Kurrum Sing, who is the reigning prince, came out, attended with a small cavalcade, to meet Major Close, who had judged it proper to travel with some appearance of State. He was in a howdah covered with plates of gold, the seat of which was a kind of chair. The other caparisons of his elephant were also superb. His nephew, a boy, rode upon another elephant, as did his Moonshee.* There were with them some gaily accoutered horsemen, and other soldiers and attendants, among whom we saw several in the Sikh costume.† The Rajah himself was dressed in a white vest, and wore a

* "Moonshee, secretary, writer."

† "Their dress is extremely scanty, a pair of long blue drawers, and a kind of chequered plaid, a part of which is fastened round the waist, and the other thrown over the shoulder, with a mean turban, form their clothing and equipage."—A Character of the Sieks, from the Observations of Col. Polier and Mr. Forster. *Asiatic Annual Register*, *Characters*, p. 10, 1802.

"They wear blue chequered clothes, and bangles or bracelets of steel round their wrists;" and, in a note to this, he adds, 'All Singhs do not wear bracelets; but it is indispensible to have steel about their persons, which they generally have in the shape of a knife or dagger.'"

red turban ornamented with jewels. He was young, very tall, and handsome, with a fine black beard, and in manner he was mild and pleasing. He is the principal Sikh Chieftain under the protection of the British authority, with a revenue amounting to thirteen or fourteen lacs of rupees nnually (£130,000 to £140,000.)

He invited us in the evening to his Court, and we were very much pleased with our visit. His Durbar consisted chiefly of Sikh Sirdars, and his Officers of State. We were also entertained with a Nautch, which was divided into three sets. The women were richly dressed in the Hindoostanee fashion; and the music, singing, and dancing were very good, though the songs we did not understand, from their being in another dialect. It is not customary to present Pawn* at this Court.

"Their name of Sikhs was changed to that of Singh by Guru Govind."—*Sir J. Malcolm's Sketch of the Sikhs*, p. 117.

* "Tamboola. The beetle leaf; but, in this place, the whole composition commonly called 'Pawn,' by the natives

The appearance of the natives in this country is much the same as that in our S. E. possessions, for the Sikh costume is not generally worn by them. Many of the women are fair, and some very beautiful.

Thermometer in the morning, 56° Fahrenheit; in the afternoon, 84°; at 9h. p.m., 64°.

30th March, *Putteeala.* We halted to-day, and again visited Kurrum Sing, the Rajah; and although we saw nothing new, for the same Sirdars were present, the same Nautch played, danced, and sung, and the same ceremony was gone through, still we returned to our tents better pleased with the Sikh Chief. He was very kind to us, and indeed paid every attention that hospitable politeness could offer. He told us also that he could shew us ex-

---

of Bengal, and beetle by the Europeans, must be understood; which every one knows is given in India by a superior as an inviolable token of friendship, favour, and protection."—*Wilkin's Translation of the Heetopades*, p. 220, note 288, 1 vol., 8vo. London, Nourse, 1787.

"Piper betle. Linn. Spec. Plant. t. 1. pars. 1, sect. 1, p. 680, spec. 154."—*Berolini.* Nauck, 1831, 8vo.

cellent lion hunting; and we regretted very much that our time did not allow us to accept of the proposal, for it would have been a novelty, and enabled us likewise to judge of the sport offered by such a kingly animal, in comparison to that of the crafty, but not less courageous tiger.

As I have already mentioned, Kurrum Sing is the Chief of the Confederated Sikhs on the South side of the Sutluj. He is perfectly independent in his own State, but is bound by his treaty to assist the British government with troops when called upon, as well as to permit supplies for the uses of our army to pass through his territory, free from all duties. Neither is he to encroach upon any of the other petty Sikh States, and thus aggrandize his power. He pays no tribute to our treasury.

I was told that Ummer Sing, who was the first of this dynasty, founded Putteeala; but I doubt this, from the appearance of the place. The present Rajah is the fifth in descent from him.

Thermometer at noon, 84° Fahrenheit.

31st March, *Moolipoor,* 10m. 4f.—Our road to-day was very good, there not being a single nullah to distress our elephants, camels, and other beasts of burden. At five miles we passed Furrudpoor, a hamlet, Putteeala bearing from thence S., 5° E. The morning was clear, and we had a beautiful view of the mountains, particularly of the Choor Pahar, which was streaked with snow, and bore N., 66° E., distant in a direct line 75 miles.

Moolipoor is a small village with a gurhee. The country around it is pretty. It was from here that we first saw the fretted crest of the Himala, but so distant, that it seemed more like a distinct reflection of mighty mountains of snow upon the deep blue ocean of the sky than any thing real. If our desires had been so much raised by the anxious wish to see these peaks, they were now increased many fold. Each moment was a feverish delay, and it was made more so, as no person could satisfy us certainly what portion of the snowy chain it was that reared itself against the high horizon. Some said that it was above Sooran, others that it was a portion of the range in Mundee, and Kooloo, but they were all undetermined, if not positively ignorant of its position. Yet we gazed upon them with all the intense feelings of travellers that have journeyed from afar, and at length behold the shrine of their adoration.

They bear, per compass, N.E., and are 120 miles distant, which gives us some idea of their immense altitude.

Thermometer, 56°, 89°, 68°, Fahrenheit.*

1st April, *Sirhind,* 10m.—We marched along a good road through an agreeable country, and passed several villages, all of them small, with the exception of Burghutpoor, which was of some size, and five miles from Moolipoor. Sirhind is embosomed among trees, and has nothing striking in its appearance as you approach it. The Choor Pahar bears N., 73° E.; and a hill near Ramnugger N., 45° E. We saw the snowy range, but it was indistinct.

Soon after our arrival, we went to the old fort, which is in a ruinous state. It is of moderate dimensions, and built of brick. In it are the

* When three registers are given, they are to be understood as made at daybreak, 3 P. M. and early in the night. ED.

tombs of Guru Govind's mother, and of his two children, who were cruelly put to death by the Turcomauns as the Mahummedans are called here. The sepulchres are very much frequented by Sikh pilgrims, and it is said that five hundred of this sect constantly perform the duties at them. The tombs are plain, and were it not for the sanctity of the dead, would be unworthy of a visit.

The history of the Sikhs is a tale of holy intolerance. Nanac their founder was a Hindoo of the Cshatriya cast.* He appears to have been a man of much piety, and great philanthrophy, and perceiving the excessive discords between the Mahummedan conquerors of India, and the natives of the country they had subjugated, he, prompted by the most benevolent motives, determined to found a religion, which should so adjust the creed of both parties, that a medium might be framed

* The second in order is the Sittri tribe, who are sometimes distinguished by the name of Kittri or Koytri. They, according to their original institution ought to be all military men; but they frequently follow other professions. Brihma is said to have produced the Kittri from his heart, as an emblem of that courage which warriors should possess.—*Dow's Hindostan.* Dissert. p. 32, vol. 1.

upon which a lesser degree of animosity, if not an absolute reconciliation, might be established. He preached forbearance and goodwill towards all men. He besought the contentious to love the One Creator, the source of peace, pleasure, and beneficence, and he promulgated this doctrine with the happiest eloquence combined with the utmost urbanity of manners.* His voice was heard during his long wanderings in all the principal cities of India, and even the enthusiastic pilgrims at Mecca and Medina, where he also went, listened with delight to the mildness of his exhortations.† After this he settled in the Punjaub and wrote a portion of what is now called the Adi Grant'h, for the guidance of his proselytes. It has since become the sacred volume of the Sikhs.‡

* Sir J. Malcolm's Sketch of the Sikhs, p. 18, 23.

† Ibid, p. 21.

‡ "That he left behind him a book, composed by himself, in verse and the language of the Punjab, but a character partly of his own invention; which teaches the doctrines of the faith he had established. That they call this character, in honour of their founder Gooroo-Mookhee: from the mouth of the preceptor. That this book, of which that standing near the altar, and several others in the hall, were

But whatever toleration might have been shewn to Nanac during his lifetime by the Mahummedan Emperors, it certainly began soon to abate when the chief direction of the new faith fell into less able hands; and upon the martyrdom of the fifth Guru, Arjunmal, the Sikhs, who had been till that period a sect of kindly men, rushed to arms, and taking Har Govind his son as their leader, they made fearful atonements with Mahummedan blood to the manes of their slaughtered Sat Guru.*

---

copies, teaches that there is but one God, omnipotent, and omnipresent, filling all space, and pervading all matter, and that he is to be worshipped and invoked; that there will be a day of retribution, when virtue will be rewarded and vice punished (I forgot to ask in what manner,) that it not only commands universal toleration, but forbids disputes with another persuasion; that it prohibits murder, theft, and such other deeds, as are, by the majority of mankind, esteemed crimes against society; and inculcates the practice of all the virtues, but particularly an universal philanthrophy, and a general hospitality to strangers and travellers."—*Observations on the Seeks and their College at Patna.* By Charles Wilkins, Esq., *in the Dissert. Relat. History and Antiquities of Asia*, vol. 2, p. 73.

* Sir J. Malcolm's Sketch of the Sikhs, p. 31 and notes, and p. 32 et seq.

The sword once unsheathed in a religious cause, fanaticism dips the consecrated banner in gore, and excites the sorrowing followers to revenge. Can we be surprised? Would not the meekest mother kill the murderer of her child, though the sacred commandment thundered in her ear, "Thou shalt not kill?" It is not at such an instant that religion is felt. Human nature draws the glittering blade, and disregards all things, till it be red and dripping from the point to the hilt, and wreathed with the warm vapour of mortality. It is only as the drops begin to curdle that it feels lassitude and repentance. Upon the death therefore of Arjunmal, who was held in the greatest reverence by the Sikhs, for he had compiled the Adi Grant'h of Nanac, and had besides added commentaries upon the most difficult passages, is it to be wondered at that they determined, from the sudden burst of natural pity, to avenge the death of their Spiritual Director, and protect their inoffensive religion even by the sacrifice of their lives?

They now became a nation; for a creed, arms, and combination, form the basis upon which the structure of Government is raised. They took possession of several villages in the Punjaub, and from these contests were the more feared, and the more persecuted. The worst incident however attending the warlike character, which was now distinctive amongst them, was schism with regard to doctrine, and faction as to the rightful succession to the office of Sat Guru, or principal spiritual leader. It occasioned feuds, which were carried on with the utmost rancour, and at length ended in the ignominious death of Tegh Bahadur, the best, but chief rival for that authority.* His son Guru Govind the most celebrated of this sect, was a man of genius and ambition. Suffering acute anguish for the loss of his father Tegh Bahadur, he ordered his followers always to wear steel, and ever bear in mind the shameful massacre of their Gurus, as well as their own personal persecutions, which the bigoted Mahummedans had made them suffer.

Aurungzeeb was at this time the Emperor of Dehli, and as Guru Govind's partizans obeyed his

* Sir J. Malcolm's Sketch of the Sikhs, p. 37, et seq.

injunctions to the letter, complaints were made to the throne, and a decree was issued, authorizing a force to pursue and seize the Guru and his attendants. It was done, and the Sikhs underwent all the terrible privations which a small number must endure when hunted and beleagured in its fastnesses.

It was in one of these places, that Guru Govind having in vain attempted to repel the assailants, gave orders to his followers to abandon the spot in the night, and separate immediately so as to ensure personal safety. Misfortune, however, was the lot of the Guru; for although he succeeded, as did many of his companions, his mother and his two children were captured, and led to Sirhind, where the Governor Foujdar Khaun cruelly put them to death.*

Govind was closely tracked, and was still unfortunate. He was with his eldest son Ajit Singh and some others blockaded in the fortress of Chamkour, where in a sally Ajit fell, fighting most gallantly.

* Sir J. Malcolm's Sketch of the Sikhs, p. 64, et seq.

After this event Govind again escaped, but of the remainder of his life, or of the manner and period of his death, nothing certain is known.* He had nevertheless left a successor who made a fearful monument of the city of Sirhind, to record the inhuman transaction it had lately witnessed.

Banda, who was a Byraggie, was the intimate friend of Govind. He was not elected to the office of Sat Guru, although the Sikhs were confederated under his command, as it had been prophesied that they should be governed by only ten Sat Gurus, and Govind was the tenth.†

The death of the Emperor Aurungzeeb, which happened about this period, left India convulsed. This was an opportunity for revenge. Banda seized it, and led the Sikhs to Sirhind, which was assaulted. Its mosques were hurled down, Foujdar Khaun the Governor was massacred, and in the wildness of fury, the dead bodies of the buried moslems were unearthed and flung for food to the throngs of vultures that glutted themselves by

* Sir J. Malcolm's Sketch of the Sikhs, p. 70.

† Ibid., p. 76, et seq.

day, and at night the wild beasts dismembered the putrefying carcases. The beautiful and luxurious city was shattered, for there is no earthquake like the stern mandate of an enraged conqueror. The wounds of nature heal. Fields bear rich produce, trees flourish, and the most delicate blossoms expand. But the disgusting scars which man leaves on the earth, are ever polluted with blood, and shunned even by his own race.

Banda after committing a series of religious atrocities, was overcome and captured. Whilst awaiting his execution at Dehli, he was told to put his child, who was sitting on his lap, to death, which he calmly did, by cutting its throat. He was then torn to pieces by red hot pincers, a death which nothing but the resolution of fanaticism could patiently inflict, or suffer.*

The invasion of Nader Shauh, and the consequent dissensions of India, which was now governed by a mockery of royalty, gave the Sikhs an opportunity to plunder far and near.

To what a state were they altered since the piety

* Sir J. Malcolm's Sketch of the Sikhs, p. 81.

of Nanac had sought to allay the irritation between the conquering and conquered creeds! We hear their founder proclaiming "Peace," we hear his followers crying "Victory attend the Guru!"* How has this resulted? From continued persecution.

When Ahmed Shauh Abdaullee had won the battle of Paneeput, he marched against the Sikhs, who upon every occasion had attacked his rear guards, and cut off the stragglers and baggage. They had also driven his son Timur Khaun, who had been sent against them, from Lahore, and in retaliation for his having filled up their sacred Tank at Umritseer, had desecrated the mosques of the city they had taken. Ahmed surprised their forces and killed 20,000 of them, and in order to suppress their unruly disposition he razed Umritseer to the ground, ordered pyramids to be made and covered with their heads, and to purify their pollution of the mosques, he commanded the walls to be washed with Sikh blood.†

* Sir J. Malcolm's Sketch of the Sikh's, p. 48.

† Ibid, p. 94, et seq.

Nevertheless he could not subdue them, and the sect continues to this day, under many petty chieftains, possessed in part of the country where it had its origin.

Sirhind, as I have already observed, is embosomed among trees, which with the Hunsla river, on the right bank of which it is situated, has contributed very much to make it a charming place. There is a brick bridge over this river, now in a rapid state of decay, but still in use. It is of considerable size, and in the construction of it, advantage has been taken of an island in the centre of the stream, which spreads considerably, is shallow and fordable; and the banks which confine it are low.

As usual we rode out in the evening, and crossing the bridge to the left bank, we soon came to a building of large size, said to have been the residence of a Durwesh, who had expended nine lacs of rupees (£90,000) upon the construction of the edifice and the gardens which it contains.

Entering by an archway in the massy wall, we found ourselves in a very extensive space of a square or oblong form, which we supposed to have been the court-yard. It is enclosed on the four sides by a high wall, with large pavilions at the corners. In the wall directly opposite to this entrance there is a handsome Dewan Khana.* After passing through the Dewan Khana we entered the centre and principal division of this princely habitation. The four sides of this portion, which is about 150 yards square, are occupied by buildings of different kinds, arranged along the sides of the basin of water which fills the entire area. A bridge leading across this basin conducts to the chief edifice, which is of several compartments. When upon the centre of the bridge, which is upon a level with the horizon, there are on each hand two Dewan Khanas. The tank is now dry. Traversing the principal edifice we came to the third, and last portion. This is a large garden, 250 yards square, ornamented with fountains, and in the wall opposite the entrance there is a handsome summer house. Without the garden and at each corner of the wall, are two fine

* State Apartment, Hall of Audience.

Mahals,* a Tukhana,† and a large circular well about 50 feet in diameter, which supplied the fountains. In the days of its beauty this must have been a paradise, such as Mahummed conceived, and this Durwesh, his follower, almost realised.‡ It had only two things wanting to make it complete, and these were the "Tooba tree," and the spring "Al Cawthar."§

* Muhul, seraglio, dwelling.

† Tukhanas are subterraneous apartments, which are used during the hot weather.

‡ "They say it is situate above the seven heavens (or in the seventh heaven) and next under the throne of God; and to express the amenity of the place tell us that the earth of it is of the finest wheat flower, or of the purest musk, or as others will have it, of saffron; that its stones are pearls and jacinths, the walls of its buildings enriched with gold and silver, and that the trunks of all its trees are of gold; among which the most remarkable is the tree called Tûba, or the tree of happiness."—*Sales Koran. Prel. Discourse*, p. 127, vol. 1. London: Clarke, 1764.

§ The righteous as the Mohummedans are taught to believe, having surmounted the difficulties, and passed the sharp bridge above-mentioned, before they enter Paradise will be refreshed by drinking at the Pond of their Prophet, who describes it to be an exact square of a month's journey in compass, its water, which is supplied by two pipes from Al Cawthar, one of the rivers of Paradise, being whiter than milk or silver, and more odoriferous than musk, with as

Leaving the residence of this princely Durwesh, we continued our ride along the banks of the Hunsla, and observed many traces of gardens surrounded by walls, besides tanks, and buildings, and concluded that we were amongst the delicious retreats of the ancient nobility of Sirhind. The green turf, and the springtide freshness of the foliage was also a novelty to us, and reminded us strongly of our native country.

We at length forded the river and entered the modern Sirhind, which is a mere provincial bazaar. Sweetmeats and spices were all that they seemed to offer for sale. We rode on for two or three miles amidst a shapeless mass of ruins, and at length came to what our guide told us was the Durwesh Hafez Rekhneh's abode, which did not at all answer to the praise bestowed upon it by Abul Fazil.* We

---

many cups set around it as there are stars in the firmament; of which water whoever drinks will thirst no more for ever. This is the first taste, which the blessed will have of their future and now near approaching felicity."—*Sale's Koran. Prel. Discourse*, p. 126, vol. 1.

* "Sehrind is a famous city, where are the delightful gardens of Hafez Rekhneh."—*Ayeen Akbery*, vol. 2, p. 107.

were convinced that our Sikh informant should have told us this at the superb residence he first shewed to us, and which I have briefly described. Hence we passed through the old fort, from one of the bastions of which there is a fine view of this desolate place, and at last arrived at our tents.

The religious and civil feuds, Banda the Byraggie, and the subsequent depredations of the Mahrattas, have not left a single building, nay, scarcely a brick of which this city appears to have beon built, entire. I have never seen such utter destruction. We were informed that the remains were twelve coss in circuit, and such might have been the extent during its greatest prosperity; but we could not, for want of time, verify the statement.

At night some nautch women danced for us, but their performance was very inferior to what we had been accustomed to.

Thermometer 57°, 89°, 68°, Fahrenheit.

2nd April, *Kant,* 10 m.—This is a small village belonging to Rajah Boop Sing of Ropoor. The country we passed through on our route was level, and well cultivated. We had no nullah to cross. Khur is ten coss, or about eleven miles on our right, for the coss hereabouts is little more than a mile. The mountains were obscured by clouds during the day, and in the evening a few drops of rain fell.

Rajah Boop Sing visited us upon our arrival here. He is a tall handsome man of about thirty years of age. Whilst strolling out in the afternoon he joined us with his hawks and dogs; for he is a great sportsman, possesses a Manton, and can shoot birds on the wing. At dinner my travelling companion received a note from him written in English, requesting a present of a bottle of cherry brandy. We were more surprised by the idiom of the letter than its contents. A Sikh chieftain upon the banks of the Sutluj writing English! Upon closer enquiry, however, we learned that one of his Mahummedan minions was the scribe of this epistle. As it would have been inconsistent with the etiquette due to Royalty to refuse, a bottle of the precious spirit was sent to him.

The Sikhs although they are prohibited by their

sacred Institutes from smoking tobacco, are allowed, as it is in accordance with charity, to give to drink and drink rejoicing.*

Churrum Sing, a Sikh Zemindar† who had been our guide at Sirhind, brought us from that place four rupees, which had been dug out of the ruins. I had given this gentleman, at his urgent solicitation, a bottle of brandy, begging of him at the same time to procure me some of the coins which are so frequently found among the remains of this capital, and he evinced his moral sense of the obligation by scrupulously drinking all the brandy, and bringing me the four rupees,

Thermometer, 64°, 89°, 74°, Fahrenheit.

* "The Sikhs are forbid the use of tobacco, (*a*) but allowed to indulge in spirituous liquors, (*b*) which they almost all drink to excess."

(*a*) The Khalasa Sikhs, who follow Nanac, and reject Guru Govind's institutions, make use of it.

(*b*) Spirituous liquors, they say, are allowed by that verse in the Adi Grant'h, which states, "Eat, and give unto others to eat. Drink, and give unto to others to drink. Be glad, and make others glad."—*Sir J. Malcolm's Sketch of the Sikhs*, p. 138.

† Zumeendar, farmer.

3rd April, *Ropoor*, 14 miles.—Soon after breaking up our camp, and approaching Ropoor this morning, we saw the snowy summits of the Himala upon the azure depths of the sky, and as the day advanced we perceived two nearer ranges, the higher of which was streaked with snow, and on the lower were the hill forts of Ramghur, Nalaghur, and Choomba. The intervening space, was a plain covered in some parts with jungle, and in others swelling into eminences.

The Rajah met us on the march, and as he was accompanied by his falconers, we diverted ourselves with hawking. It was a beautiful sight, and reminded us strongly of those romantic days, when the chivalry of Europe indulged in this exciting pastime, for there were numerous attendants variously costumed, many spirited horses, and falconers with the hawks ready leashed. We were soon galloping after the quarry, which consisted of hares, partridge, and quails.

It was animating to see the Churruck flown at the hares, trying to stoop, but unsuccessful, cancelleering and following their mazy courses amongst the low brushwood. Now a partridge, or a quail would rise fluttering, and sweep along, and as rapidly the Bassee was hurled—a moment —and the quarry was struck, and we shouted loudly, and dashed forwards with a slackened bridle to reclaim. The Churruck was unsuccessful in its stoops at the hares, but by hovering over them gave the Rajah's dogs an opportunity to run them down.

There were besides other kinds of hawks, which were flown at partridges and quails, and were equally sure as the Bassee. Only one oı two of the leash were lost, and they, from some check, raked.

The Bassee and the Churruck were two species we had never seen before. The former is rather larger than the Tirumptee, which is so small that it is always held in the hand and thrown like a stone at small birds, such as quails, doves, minas, &c. The latter is large and sluggish, and is quarried at hares.

We crossed two dry nullahs to-day, and remarked a great deficiency of cultivation. Our tents were pitched close to the ferry over the Sutluj, upon a pleasant spot of ground, with a splendid view of the mountains in front.

Ropoor is the residence of the Rajah, but it is a miserable little town on a low line of eminences. Upon the opposite bank of the Sutluj is the Punjaub, or country of the Five Waters.* Along that side is a range of dwarfish hills, which rises immediately from the river, and skirts it.

Boop Sing upon our arrival sent us a basket containing strawberries, peas, celery, and cabbage, the produce of his garden, and with them a much greater rarity, a few pounds of ice. He does not however improve upon acquaintance, as he wants a proper sense of dignity and manner, and in his enthusiasm to imitate our English customs, has like all foreigners, by some mistake chosen the worst.

* The following are the names of the five rivers:—
Beyah or Hyphasis.
Ravee or Hydraotes.
Chenaub or Acesines.
Jelum or Hydaspes.
Sind or Indus.

He has about sixty villages under his control, which yield him a lac of rupees (£10,000) annually, but his country is very badly managed, and one of the people of the town told me, that his officers were—verily, sad rascals.

In the afternoon we were invited to see the Sutluj netted, and a large quantity of fish was caught. After this we bathed in it and crossed over into the Punjaub. The stream at the ferry is rapid, and 550 yards wide.

This evening we were very much pleased with the performance of four men who came to our tents and sung many songs accompanied with a guitar. Some sets of Nautch girls also came, but as our time was precious, we were reluctantly obliged to dismiss them.

This celebrated class of women in India, is rapidly decreasing both in numbers and talent. Their origin dates from the most ancient times. We can easily conceive, that in the early ages of mankind, when there was less reserve, that after the celebration of holy rites, many of those who were present, would, from real joy, be inspired with great enthusiasm. This would lead to the institution of festivals after all solemn occasions. As pure religion declined, the emanations of mental gratitude would soon be changed into material gratifications, and the throng of happy singers and dancers would give place to a chosen band, which would then perform the additional established ceremonies. The loveliest maidens would be selected by crafty Hierophants, and instructed purposely in every grace that might fascinate the senses. The rich and powerful among the concourse would require possession, and in order that no imputation might arise, theories would be promulgated, which would teach the ignorant multitude, and ignorance is always led by the medium of the senses, to offer sacrifices to the Productive Powers of Nature. By these artifices a system would be founded, concerning the iniquity of which history bears certain testimony, though veiled in mysterious words.* The consequent to this would be an increase of priestesses for these

* Maurice's Indian Antiquities. Dissert. 2, p. 336, et seq.

orgies. Princes would require them at court during sacred festivities, and we can be certain that the example would be quickly followed by the nobles.

During the magnificent reigns of the early Hindoo Rajahs these Nautch girls, or Bayaderes, officiated in the temples of Siva and Parvati,* and in the later dynasty of the Moghul Emperors they formed a part of the royal State.† They were chosen from the most beautiful children, and while the rest of their sex grew up in natural ignorance, they were taught every accomplishment that could give an attractive power to the mind, or add to the graces of a person that was already exquisite in its native simplicity. From the circumstance

* Maurice's Indian Antiquities. Dissert. 2, p. 933, et seq.

† "Chah Jehan was not content only to have them come to the seraglio at those feasts, but when they came to salute him, according to that ancient custom that obligeth them to come every Wednesday to do obeyance to the King in the Amkas, &c."

Bernier's Letter to M. de la Mothe le Vayer, containing a description of Dehli and Agra.

of their being with the court, their manners were polished. They had likewise a great share in the political intrigues of the country. In short they possessed extensive influence, and from their attainments it cannot be doubted, that, although they did not advance the morality, they nevertheless tended very much to improve the habits of all ranks.

The overthrow of the Moghul empire, the revolutions which succeeded, and our subsequent conquests, and introduction of foreign customs, have lessened their numbers and popularity. Still, they are to be seen at every native court, and frequently attend the marriage ceremonies of those who can afford to remunerate them.

Thermometer, 76°, 92°, 72°, Fahrenheit.

Bearings by the compass from Ropoor.

Choor Pahar .... S. 84° E.
Nalaghur Fort .. N. 72° E.
Ramghur Fort .. N. 61° E.
Chumba Fort .. N. 34° E.
Moorkur Fort .. N. 30° E.
Peak near Subahtoo .. E.

4th April, *Plasseea*, 8m.—Plasseea is a village with a small fort on the right bank of the Sursa river. It was formerly the residence of the Rajah Ram Sing, who has, since, made Nalaghur the capital of his little state.

The road this morning was very good. The storm which had been gathering for the last two or three days, at length burst upon us early in the noon, which made the air cool and pleasant. Some hail fell with the rain.

In the afternoon, Rajah Ram Sing visited Major Close. He is of the Chundail* tribe of Raujpoots, between sixty and seventy years old, and is, in manners, mild and agreeable. He told us that his ancestors had inhabited this part of the country for the last five hundred years. His state yields him a revenue of 75,000 rupees (£7,500), one third of which is paid in money, and the remainder in produce.

* The Chundaila, classed by some of the genealogists amongst the thirty-six tribes, were powerful in the twelfth century, possessing the whole of the regions between the Jumna and Nerbudda.—*Tod's Annals of Rajast'han*, vol. 1, p. 116. London, Smith & Co., 1829, 2 vols. 4to.

When he left us, we strolled out to the high banks of the Sursa, to admire the magnificent prospect before us, at leisure.

Thermometer, 72°, 68°, 68°, Fahrenheit.

5th April, *Nalaghur.*—The road to-day was excellent, passing through a most lovely country. Nalaghur is a small stone fort upon an eminence of considerable height, which is part of a range of hills that rise above it, to a further elevation of 700 or 800 feet, forming a strong pass into the mountainous district of Hindoor. The town is of moderate size, and has a pretty appearance in this hilly scene. The road approaching it, lies through stony hollow ways and a thick jungle of bamboos which covers the bases of these ranges.

In the Nepaul war of 1814, Nalaghur was, together with Taraghur, a small post dependent upon it, occupied by the Goorkas, under the command of Chumra Rana.* It was the first fort

* The British General, resolving to put nothing to hazard, made a road with great labour, and sat himself down, with his heavy guns, before Nalagurh, on the 1st November. Having breached the wall, the garrison surrendered on the 5th, capitulating also for the stockade on the same ridge,

taken by the Division under the personal command of Sir D. Ochterlony, during his advance against Ummer Sing's positions in this portion of the Nepaul territories. After a practicable breach had been made by two eighteen pounders it capitulated. Ramghur, which was another fort in the possession of the Goorkas at that time, does not appear to be above five miles distant, in a direct line.

Rajah Ram Sing's Dewan* was very communicative, and amongst other circumstances told us that a body of Chundail Raujpoots who went on a pilgrimage to Jawallajee, on the Beyah or Hyphasis, were pleased with the country there, and settled in it. They by degrees dispossessed the original inhabitants of their lands, and became the masters. The present Rajah is descended from them.

---

called Taragurh."—*History of the Political and Military Transactions in India, &c.*, by H. T. Prinsep, vol. 1, p. 105. London, Kinsbury & Co., 1825, 2 vols. 8vo.

* Dewan, Minister.

6th April, *Nalaghur.*—We halted to-day, in order to make preparations for our journey to Malown and Belaspoor. We therefore left our elephants, camels, and large tents, together with the greater number of our attendants, under the protection of our kind friend Rajah Ram Sing, and for the first time got ready our Bechobas, light tents, ten feet square.

7th April, *Ramghur,* 9m. 4f., elevation 4,054 feet.—We marched this morning at a quarter past six, and reached our Bechobas at 10 A.M. The road was the one made by the Pioneers for Sir D. Ochterlony's advance to Malown. It is from ten to twelve feet wide, even and good, but leading through a country which had presented the most formidable obstacles. Rocks had been blasted, trees cut down, parapets built along the edges of precipitous declivities, but the skill and perseverance of our engineer and pioneer officers had surmounted every difficulty, and for the first time, the deep glens of the Himala echoed the rolling of the heavy breaching guns. The only difficult part now, however, is that which leads down into the ravine below Ramghur, through which the Chicknee river rushes, and the ascent of full 1000 feet to the village under the fort.

Ramghur is a good mountain village, and has afforded abundant supplies to our camp, which consists of sixty or seventy persons.

The scenery around is picturesque, but not sublime. The sides of the mountains are well cultivated. The fields consist of a succession of terraces, rising one above another like vast flights of steps, which has a novel and striking effect. The hamlets are very numerous, many of them perched upon points from 1500 to 2000 feet above the bases of the hills. The pine is abundant, and it is the first European tree that we have seen. In the evening we walked up to the fort, which is on a small peak about 400 feet above our tents, and from 500 to 600 yards to the right of the battery from whence it was breached, which is on a level with it, and which in two days drove the enemy out of their stronghold. I should have supposed it almost impossible to have drawn guns up to such a position. The fort when in possession of the Goorkas was a mere oblong of small dimensions, and too weak to resist the fire of heavy artillery.

The view from here was magnificent. In one direction were the snowy mountains, the Choor Pahar, Baree Daybee, Malown, Soorujghur, and Bahadoorghur; in the opposite we looked down upon our tents at Nalaghur, recognised Plasseea and Ropoor beyond, and saw the Sutluj and Surpun winding far along the plains, and fading in the distance. The Punjaub, the country left of the Sutluj, and indeed all that portion, seemed like an exquisite map spread out beneath us.

It was on the Ramghur range that we first met with raspberry bushes, and what a host of early recollections did they bring, to say nothing of crimson-smeared faces and jam.

Malown bore from here N. ¼ E. about 10 miles in direct distance. The Choor Pahar was E. by S. We received our letters from Subahtoo to-day, which gave us great pleasure.

Thermometer, 64°, 80°, 64°, Fahrenheit.

8th April, *Sahee,* 8m.—We started at forty

minutes past 5, A.M., and got to our Bechobas at 9 o'clock. Shortly after leaving Ramghur we crossed the Coauj river, the road leading to it is down a deep and rapid descent. From hence the ground was level till we reached a spot above the Gumbur river, the descent to which was long and sharp, and covered with wood. The prospect from here was beautiful. Continuing our ride up, and in the river which flows swiftly and is from forty to sixty yards wide, for a considerable distance, we at length began to ascend the wooded hill on the opposite side by a steep and difficult road, and shortly reached our tent at Sahee.

Upon the whole, the route was difficult for artillery. The country we passed through was, for a mountainous district, open. It was well cultivated, and very picturesque. My Arab fell down a precipitous bank to-day, but most fortunately neither horse nor rider received any injury.

Just before us is the razed fort of Soorujghur, upon a high part of the Malown range, and distant about three miles. It is 1100 feet above our tents, and 4927 feet above the sea. Sergeant Gordon passed us at this place on his way from Subahtoo to Malown. His wife was in a Chumpala or Hill Litter, which was carried by eight bearers.

The Chumpaun, or as it is more frequently called, the Chumpala, is the usual vehicle in which persons of distinction, especially females, are carried, when travelling amongst these mountains. The body of it is a square or oblong frame made of split bamboos, with a pentroof-top of the same material, and the whole is generally covered with white or red cloth. It is barely sufficient for a person to lie in. To the sides at the bottom, two stout bamboo poles are fastened, which are twelve or more feet in length, by which it is carried in different ways by the hill porters according to the nature of the road; and as the ascents and descents are very frequent, and steep, a contrivance has been resorted to, in order to ease the labour of bearing it in one particular position. This is done by a cord tied across the poles at each end of the Chumpala, in the centre of which cord also, is fastened a shorter bamboo pole, which being moveable in every direction, forms an axle upon the shoulders of the bearers as they stand before each other, by which all sudden jerks are avoided, as it allows the body of the machine to sway to and fro. As the road happens to be either easy or difficult, eight, twelve, or sixteen persons are requisite for one Chumpala, some of whom in dangerous places walk beside it, to steady it.

The Chumpalas which are used by females of distinction, are covered with the finest scarlet broad-cloth, richly embroidered with gold or silver, and the ends of the bamboo poles are likewise ornamented with gilt knobs. They also shut close, to screen the person entirely from the sight of the inquisitive. There is another conveyance which is much more in use than the Chumpala. This is the Doolee. It is merely a hammock, fastened to a strong bamboo pole, and is carried upon the shoulders of two or four men.

Subahtoo is 19 m. 4 f. distant from Sahee. Irkee is 12 coss.

Around us are numerous small hamlets and detached houses, which give a very pretty effect to the view.

In the evening I took my gun and strolled out, and got two shots, both of which were successful. One was at a Kosla or Hill Pheasant, and the other at a Koorkee or Jungle Hen. I was very much pleased with having killed the Kosla, as it reminded me of the common Pheasant in England.

Thermometer, 54°, 78°, 64°, Fahrenheit.

9th April, *Fort of Malown*, 9 m., elevation 4,448 ft.*—At 5 H. 25 M. A. M., we commenced our journey, and arrived at our Bechobas at 10 A. M. The road was good, lying through the valley formed by the Malown and Bahadoorghur ridges, until we came opposite to the Fort, when we descended to the bed of the Gumbur and from thence began to ascend the enormous side

* All the elevations, unless otherwise specified, are above the sea level. Also, the ascents and descents refer to perpendicular height.—Ed.

of the mountain. It took me one hour, unencumbered as I was, to climb from here to the summit, from which circumstance a slight idea may be formed of the excessive fatigue our Troops, all of them Seapoys, must have undergone in dragging up the eighteen pounders, in the front of a most fierce and devoted enemy, in order to demolish their last stronghold. There is another crooked path which also leads to the Fort, up which we might have ridden our horses, but that we lost our way, and they were in consequence sent by the made road, and did not reach our little Camp before 12 o'clock. The prospects from many places on our route were beautiful.

Our Bechobas are perched upon the crest of the Malown hills, between the Fort and the breaching battery erected by Sir David Ochterlony. The ridge here is only twenty-two yards wide, with valleys on either hand 2000 feet deep, through one of which the Gumbrola rolls; through the other the Gumbur. Belaspoor on the Sutluj lies before and beneath us upon a level piece of ground, hemmed in by hills. It appears not more than ten miles distant.* The horizon beyond it is the Snowy range, which seems only thirty miles distant, although in reality it is considerably further. The space which intervenes is a succession of lofty mountains, teeming with every variety of light and shade, like vast broken waves. In an opposite direction are the Ramghur heights topped with the ruins of little stockades, over which we see the glowing plains around Sirhind. What adds much likewise to the beauty of this splendid scene, is the cultivation on the flanks of the valleys. The terraced fields are like the steps of some magnificent amphitheatre, upon which the produce waves in many hues. These terraces are carried up to the tops of the ranges, and frequently in situations, apparently inaccessible. Many elegant little hamlets are scattered up and down amongst the fields, and upon the peaks are several small forts, while here and there large pinewoods sweep down in rich dark green masses, intersected by thin rills of

* All the distances given are in a direct line, unless otherwise specified.—Ed.

the whitest foam or long forky mountain paths. There is, too, an amenity and perfume in the air, and repose, which sooths the senses, while the immensity of the view expands the mind, and makes it contemplate all with the purest of pleasures, natural devotion.

It was in the midst of this scene of sublimity that the most arduous operations of the Goorka war occurred. There may be many opinions as to the policy of this war, but there can be only one as to the conduct of the parties engaged in it, and that is unhesitating praise.

Upon the plains of India, our troops had constantly acted upon the offensive, and had been as constantly victorious, but among these enormous dells and craggy heights, a fearless enemy rushed headlong upon them, and forced them to combat under a series of novel emergencies. Consequently every triumph gained by us, was marked by a display of skill and fortitude almost unparalleled.

The frontier which was penetrated at different points by the invading columns, was about 600 miles in extent. It is, however, only the extreme west of this line, bounded by the Sutluj, which it is here necessary to describe. Sir David Ochterlony with a division consisting of 6000 men exclusively Native Infantry, and artillery composed of two eighteen pounders, ten six pounders, and four mortars and howitzers, advanced from Loodeeanah against Ummer Sing's defences on the Ramghur and Malown ranges.* By a succession of masterly movements and attacks, Nalaghur and Ramghur were taken, and the Goorka Chief with extreme anger found himself surrounded on the fortified heights of Malown, and

* Prinsep's Transactions in India, vol. 1, p. 83.

" Staff of the Army which invaded the Nepalese Province of Hindur in 1814, under the command of Major-General David Ochterlony.

Major of Brigade..........Capt. Edmund Cartwright.
Officiating Aid-de-Camp . Lieut. Peter Lawtie.
Field Engineer & Surveyor . Lieut. Peter Lawtie.
Assistant ditto ditto........Ens. George Hutchinson.
Assist. Commissary General. Lieut. Alex. Bannerman.
Sub-Assistant ditto ....Lieut. Sneyd.

Commanding the Line ....Brigadier John Arnold.
" " Reserve ..Lieut.-Col. A. Thompson.
" " Artillery ..Major Alex. Mc'Leod."

Sketches of the Goorka War.

cut off from his supplies. A party, too, under the command of Colonel Thompson had seized Deontul, the most important point upon the Malown ridge.

Upon this Ummer Sing's affairs became urgently difficult, and Buktee Tappa the favourite leader of the Goorkas, who had been stationed at Senj, perceiving that his position there was useless, forsook it, and entered Malown at night. A council was held upon the spot, and as the dislodgement of Colonel Thompson was absolutely necessary, it was determined to make an assault upon his post. Buktee, with the patriotism of a mountaineer, offered to lead, and either take the place or perish. Daybreak was to be the signal for the attack. The occasion was solemn. Buktee took leave of his wives, whom he told to prepare for the Suttee, and, what was yet more trying, of his infant son, whom he intrusted, under the most sacred assurances of fulfilment to the care of Ummer Sing. Such moments are indeed full of anxiety. The past, the present, and the future, meet as it were upon a spot of time, for one instant, and then bid farewell to each other for ever!

The arrangements for the attack being completed, the Goorkas silently issued from Malown, and formed in a semi-circle below Deontul, which Colonel Thompson had hastily fortified, with guns placed at the weakest points to command the approaches to his position. At length the gray hues of dawn were observed, and the distant summits of the snowy range blushed in the light of morning. The long trumpets of the Goorkas sounded fiercely, mingled with frantic yells, and they rushed with drawn swords from all parts up to the attack. Our men were on the alert to meet them. The guns loaded with grape-shot, volley after volley, swept away those that advanced. The Goorkas nevertheless pushed on undauntedly. In a few minutes the whole place was shrouded in a pall of white smoke, braided with the glittering flashes of musketry, while the loud thunders of the artillery pealed in echoing death-knells through the deep and distant glens of the Himalaya. Still they made charge after charge, but were unable to accomplish their purpose, and having lost an enormous number of men, they began to falter. Colonel Thompson perceiving this, immediately ordered the Seapoys to leave the works and charge with the bayonet, which they did most gallantly, driving all before them. The enemy retreated to Malown. After the close of this bloody struggle, the field was searched, and the body of the noble, but unfortunate Buktee Tappa was found among the heaps of slain. It was wrapped in a shawl as a mark of high esteem and respect, and sent to Ummer Sing.

On the following day preparations were seen for some great ceremony. It was for the Suttee. Between the opposing and opposed armies, the two widows of Buktee Tappa burned themselves with the corpse of their husband, showing as much affection for the fallen hero, as he had himself manifested heroism in his desperate attack on Deontul.* There is much in the pomp

* Military Sketches of the Goorka War in India in the years 1814, 1815, 1816, p. 24, et seq. 1 vol. 8vo. R. Hunter, London, 1822.

and circumstance of war; there is more in the dauntless courage of the warrior, but the devotion of the patriot surpasses the expression of language!

After this repulse, a breaching battery was made to reduce the Fort of Malown, which was effected in a few days, and Ummer Sing capitulated.

We were conducted through the fort in the evening by Serjeant Gordon, who has charge of the guns and stores, and who paid us every attention. It is a small, intricate, strongly built piece of masonry; but guns once established in Sir D. Ochterlony's battery, would quickly scatter it in fragments to the winds. From here we walked to the spot from whence it was breached, which is situated about 400 yards to the southward. We then went to Narrain Kote, a stockaded post about 400 or 500 yards still further to the south. It was from here that Buktee Tappa issued to storm Colonel Thompson's position at Deontul. Here he had trodden with the firm elasticity of manhood, and near it, had fallen with honour on the field of glory! Who would not have felt a warrior, on the spot? Deontul is on a lower point of this ridge about 800 yards onwards still to the south, and at the end of it is the Fort of Soorujghur. We returned to our tents in admiration of all that we had seen, and with mingled feelings of pride and regret. Pride that we had been victors; regret for the Goorka hero!

Thermometer 49°, 81°, 60°, Fahrenheit.

10th April, *Belaspoor,* 10m. 4f., elevation 1465 feet.—Descending northwards from the Fort, we passed the spot where Captain Showers was killed, which is midway between Malown and the village at the base of the mountain. From this village we ascended to Ruttunghur, which was Colonel Arnold's post. It is to the north, and almost as high as Malown. Four or five hundred yards to the East of Ruttunghur are the tombs of Captain Showers, and Lieutenant Lawtie of the Engineers.* There is a neat monument erected

* "In the columns of diversion under Captains Showers and Bowyer, I have to express my entire approbation of the

over the grave of Captain Showers. A cold thrill, such as the appearance of an unwelcome messenger causes, ran to my heart whilst I traced with my finger upon the marble slab the following inscription.

"Sacred to the memory of Charles Lionel Showers, late Captain of the 1st Battalion, 19th Regiment, Bengal Native Infantry, killed whilst gallantly storming the Malown heights, 15th April, 1815. Aged 34 years, 6 months, and 5 days."

---

conduct of Captain Bowyer and of Lieutenant Rutledge; on whom the command devolved; and to lament the loss of a most zealous, brave, and excellent officer in Captain Showers, who fell gallantly setting an example of heroism to his men, which might have been of the utmost importance, had not his death, at a most critical moment, staggered his troops and given confidence to the enemy."—p. 592. *Papers respecting the Nepaul War*, printed for the Proprietors of East India Stock. 3rd March, 1824.

"A Goorka officer considerably before his men was at this time approaching, and Showers hastening to meet him, a single combat took place in which he slew his adversary, on the space that yet separated the contending parties. Scarcely had this act of personal bravery been achieved when Showers was shot, and fell dead."—*Military Sketches of the Goorka War*, p. 25.

I knew him when in the hey-day of his youth!

A rude tomb of stones is all that marks the burial place of poor young Lawtie, whose unabating enterprise, and intuitive perception of difficulties, combined with the best method of surmounting them, had most contributed, next to the commanding and persevering genius of Sir David Ochterlony, in lightening the soldier's fatigues, and leading him on to victory.* Any attempt to praise Sir

* "Lieutenant Lawtie accompanied the night movement, and evinced his usual zeal and indefatigable activity; and it is to the intelligent mind, the diligent inquiry, and personal observation of this officer, that I feel indebted for the knowledge which enabled me to have the outlines of a plan which has been crowned with greater, more important, and earlier success, than my most sanguine expectations had anticipated, as the result has terminated in the evacuation of the Fort of Loorryghur and all the Southern dependent stockades."—*Papers respecting the Nepaul War*, p. 593.

"Major General Ochterlony mentions with peculiar applause the conduct of Lieutenant Colonel Thomson, of Captain Showers who fell in the action, and of the late Lieutenant Lawtie of the Engineers, whose services, not on this occasion only (referring to Malown), but throughout the campaign, were of transcendent merit and utility, and had obtained the repeated acknowledgements of Major

David would be to presume that upon throwing a handful of water into the ocean, it would break its bounds by such addition. It took us an hour and a half to walk from Malown to the tombs. Descending to the Gumbur river from Ruttunghur, and crossing it, we joined our horses, sent by another road, at the hamlet of Raujpoora, where Major Close was met by a Deputation from Maha Chund the Rajah of Belaspoor. Five or six miles more, over a bad stony road, brought us to our Bechobas.

Belaspoor has a neat Bazar, which is not however overstocked with merchandise. The town is paved with large round stones, which to a person

---

General Ochterlony and the Commander-in-Chief. The untimely death of this promising young officer. by an illness occasioned by excessive fatigue in the execution of his duty, has been deplored by the Government and the Army."—*Secret Letter from Lord Moira.* Dated 20th July, 1815. *Papers respecting the Nepaul War*, p. 756.

"To record its sense of Lieutenant Lawtie's services, the army went into mourning; and afterwards erected a monument to his memory in the Cathedral Church of Calcutta."—*Sketches of the Goorka War*, p. 33.

unaccustomed to such footing renders the streets very disagreeable, and much more so to horsemen. Every fifth person we saw here had a goitre.

On the opposite bank of the Sutluj towards the Snowy Chain, are the petty States of Sookaid, Mundee, Kooloo, and Chumba. Mundee is reported to be a considerable Rauj, exporting large quantities of iron and woollen cloth.

We have just been visited by Rajah Maha Chund of Kullowr. He is a poor, emaciated looking person of the Chundail tribe of Raujpoots, and appears of mild manners. He complains of the encroachments of the Sikh, Runjit Sing, the powerful ruler of the Punjaub.

In the evening we walked to the residence of Dabey Chund, the father of the present Rajah. It commands a fine view of the town and the whole of the valley. There is near, a well of the finest water. It is an oblong of thirty feet by twenty feet. The more we see of this lower mountain country the more we are charmed with it.

In the evening we wiled away the time, which

was insufferable from the heat, by a Nautch. The women were dressed in the Hindoostanee fashion, and being poor proficients were tiresome: yet we could not refuse their attendance, as it is always supposed to be an appendage of rank, without losing much of our consequence in the eyes of the natives. But it was not the heat only, nor the Nautch women which rendered the time disagreeable, nay insupportable; we had to receive and pay visits of ceremony, and to suffer also crowds of idlers to remain in our camp for the purpose of gratifying curiosity. The prevailing rock at Belaspoor is a very coarse Puddingstone.

Thermometer 57°, 97°, 66°, Fahrenheit.

11th April, *Bojoon* or *Pijoon,* 9m.—This is a small hamlet on the right bank of the Gumbur river, immediately below Malown. We returned to Raujpoora, by the same route that we had traversed yesterday. The road was stony and bad, particularly near Belaspoor. From a spot on the way hither, close to the town, I threw a stone almost across the stream of the Sutluj, but the breadth of the river at Belaspoor is about 300 yards, and it is unfordable. I purchased a Goont or Hill Pony for forty-five rupees.

Thermometer 63°, 77°, 68°, Fahrenheit.

12th April, *Sahee*, 9m.—Left this morning at 5 H. 30 M., and reached the Bunneea's shop* here at 9 H. 50 M. A. M. We dismounted at the Peepul† tree which is about two miles from this place, and from the ruined terrace around it admired the lovely view, bounded by the snowy chain of the

* Bunneeas' shops supply provisions of all kinds.

† "From the fondness of birds for the fruit, and the tenacity of life in the seed of two species, Ficus indica and religiosa, are explained two phenomena very familiar to all who have visited India; one is that of a palm-tree growing out of the centre of the Banyan; and the other that of the pippul, F. religiosa, vegetating (where the seed has been deposited in cracks), on the driest walls and most elevated domes and minarets, which by its increase, it soon destroys." —*Royle's Illustrations of the Botany, &c., of the Himalayan Mountains, and the Flora of Cashmere*, p., 339. London: Allen & Co., 1839. 1 vol. folio.

"ARUN.—Some Kshetriya lad, who here awhile pursues
His sacred studies.
JAN.—You have rightly judged
His birth: for see * * *
* * * * * in one hand he bears
The pipal staff."

Wilson's Hindu Theatre, vol. 1, p. 346.

Himala. The peepul tree is on a low ridge which connects the Malown and Bahadoorghur lines of heights.

Sahee is on an elevated spot, and commands a fine prospect to the S. E.

Soorujghur bears S. W. by W. ½ W., and is 2m. 6f. distant.

Thermometer 58°, 83°, 68°, Fahrenheit.

13th April, *Ramghur Fort*. 8m. 4f.—About 2m. 6f. from Sahee, we descended into the bed of the Gumbur river, and rode nearly a mile in it before we ascended to the left bank. The enormous ravine through which this river rolls, is one of those, where the wildness of the rocky heights is so gracefully combined with the solemn calmness of the woods; where the full tones of the brilliantly clear mountain stream, rise so lightly through the purer air to the intensely azure dome of the sky, that the mind is filled with a succession of happy thoughts, and we feel inspired with the wish to be spirits of airy mould, rather than what we are, to wander through it with more exquisite sensibility, than that of mere mortality.

The Choor Pahar and the Snowy Chain were in sight all day. The former is still covered with snow. Kumlaghur bears N. ¼ W., distant forty miles, and Soorujghur N. N. E. ½ E. five miles.

Our evening walk was to within a mile of the razed Fort of Jorjooroo, which is upon the same ridge as Ramghur. We went by the road made during the late war for the artillery, and found it excellent. The wind was deliciously cool.

Thermometer 58°, 88°, 62¼°, Fahrenheit.

14th April, *Nalaghur,* 9m, 4f.—The prospect from Ramghur this morning before daybreak, impressed us deeply with the magnificence of this extraordinary country. Before sunrise, the Choor Pahar, the mountains far beyond it, and the lofty Himalaya, were of a dark blue, a heaving, but noiseless ocean, the outlines of whose vast waves were sharply defined. As the sun rose, this uniform hue faded away, and the majestic snowy range dazzled us with its resplendency, whilst the dependent hills seemed to rejoice in the varied beauty of their rich verdures. The massive Ridge of snow did not show any particular towering peak, or broad sweep of table-land, but was irregular, curiously rugged, and magically distinct; one of the noblest aspects possible to behold.

The snowy chain bore N. by E. to N. by W. At 5 H. 5 M. A. M, we left this sublime view with great regret, and during our descent to the Chicknee nullah, which occupied fifty minutes, got many fine glimpses of the ruined fort above us. We reached our camp at about 9 H. 30 M. A. M.

We were glad to find our people in excellent health and spirits, and they all spoke highly of the civility they had experienced from the inhabitants of Nalaghur.

Thermometer: extremes 56°, 94°, Fahrenheit.

15th April. We halted to-day. Thermometer: highest $97\frac{3}{4}°$ Fahrenheit.

16th April, *Buddeea*, 10m.—We found the road, which lay through a valley varying from one to three miles in width, very good. The hills on the right are about 100 feet high. They are a continuation of those at Ropoor, and seem to be of the same formation.

Buddeea is a hamlet on the Sursa river, belonging to the Rajah of Nalaghur. Thus far the valley is well cultivated. The corn is nearly ripe, indeed in some places it is cut.

Thermometer: extremes 72°, 90°, Fahrenheit.

17th April, *Pinjore,* 11m., elevation 1900 feet.—We continued our march along the valley, which was more wooded than before, but the road was not so good. About 4f. from Buddeea we crossed the Sursa.

It rained almost the whole way, and completely drenched all our party.

We received very kind letters from our friends at Subahtoo, and also from Captain Lumsdaine, who, besides, sent us a dozen mules from Hurdwar.

Thermometer: extremes 70°, 66°, Fahrenheit.

18th April. Halted. It rained all last night, and the greater part of to-day, but towards the evening the weather having cleared up, we walked to a large well, which is resorted to as a place of worship by the Hindoos. There is nothing particular about it, being merely an old ruinous building, with images, and shady trees. It is of great antiquity.

We next proceeded to a most delightful place. It is a garden which has been laid out on the natural slope of the ground in six separate and successive terraces, one below another. A canal about ten feet wide of the clearest water runs through the centre. In this is a line of fountains extending from the entrance to the end, abundantly supplied with water from the hills above, which flows through the canal, and falls in Chuddurs or broad cascades from terrace to terrace. Behind these crystal curtains there are recesses for lamps, which are lit during nights of festivity. Similar lines of fountains branch off on the right and left to other parts of the garden. In the centre is an artificial tank, and in the middle of it a small Mahal surrounded with fountains, which during the hot months must be a delicious retreat. A profusion of roses, with other flowers, shrubs, and handsome trees ornament this beautiful spot. The gardens of Shalimar, at the Tauj Mahal, Secundra, Sirhind, have perhaps equalled this in profuseness of bloom, or gracefulness of arrangement, but this surpasses them in the charms which Nature herself has bestowed; for from the Mahal there is an enchanting view, the valley on one side being closed by high mountains crested with dark green pines, and overspread with woods, rich fields, rocks, hamlets and hill forts, while nearer heights covered with jungle of all shades broken by shreds of culture, and dotted with the circular towers of gurhees, and numerous villages, partially hide it on the other side from the plains which are occasionally seen between the gaps in the range, and now covered with the ruddy golden haze of sunset. The valley itself is thickly wooded, although in parts there is cultivation, and it is besides richly diversified by the tall, broken banks of the Kosilla which runs through it, adding a thousand smiles to this re-created Eden. In short nothing is wanting, that may give happiness to the mind, but the absence of that visionary and incoherent desire, which when novelty is past, causes a void in the heart, and harshly convinces us, that although we are in the midst of beauty in this world, our creation is imperfect.

These gardens were made by some Mahummedan, but are now, together with Pinjore, in the possession of the Rajah of Putteeala. They have become almost a wilderness, but I am happy to say that our friend the Sikh Chieftain, Kurrum Sing, is endeavouring to restore them to their former beauty.

Bearings.

Fort at Bauhr......N. 12° E. 7 miles.

Tuksal ....N. 33° E. 6 miles.

Thermometer: extremes 62°, 76°, Fahrenheit.

19th April, Halted.—In the evening we revisited the gardens, and made a rough measurement of their extent.

From the entrance to the	first fall..	112	paces.
"	second fall	100	"
"	third fall..	117	"
"	fourth fall	136	"
"	fifth fall ..	76	"
"	sixth & end	100	"
	Total length	641	
Width of the garden beyond the Mahal		386	

We had a very good Nautch last night. The women danced in a peculiar style, and sung a good collection of songs. They were not handsome, and their dress did not differ from that of the Hindoostanee Nautch girls.

Thermometer: extremes 64°, 82°, Fahrenheit.

20th April, *Bauhr,* 7m. 4f., elevation 2500 feet. —We travelled upon an excellent road which lay through jungle, and was very winding. The morning was extremely fresh and pleasant, which after the heat of the plains was most renovating. On the route we met the Rajah of Naan returning with his bride from the mountains. He was accompanied by a retinue of many hundred persons of all ranks and denominations, and in a very handsome Chumpala covered with scarlet cloth, and profusely ornamented with gold, his young wife was carried, followed by her female relatives and attendants in other Chumpauns. They, together with horsemen gaily attired bearing many-coloured flags, Falconers with hawks, rude music, elephants, camels, Palkees,* Hill Porters with

* The well known Palankeen.

northern countenances, and a host of fine goats, sheep, and dogs, formed a splendid pageant in the midst of this beautiful scene. The bride we were told was the daughter of the Rajah of Kytul.

Bauhr is a small hamlet, with a Bunneea's shop and a store-house. Although situated at the foot of the hills, it is still sufficiently elevated to command a fine view of the Pinjore valley, and, beyond the low range of hills the haze-covered plains. We can distinguish the ground upon which we pitched our tents at Ropoor, and the swelling eminences which skirt the Sutluj.

Our travelling equipment must now undergo another change, for the camels cannot proceed further, and the elephants, perhaps, only as far as Subahtoo. All this affords abundant matter among our good-natured followers for learned theory and most abstruse controversy.

21st April. Halted.

22nd April, *Subahtoo,* 13m. 1f., elevation 4205 feet.—Shortly after leaving Bauhr we began to ascend the mountains, by a road which had been constructed by Pioneers. It was excellent, but very winding, in order to diminish the difficulty of the ascent.

The thrilling elasticity caused by the pureness of the air, and the irresistible impulses of curiosity to see this extraordinary country, are quite inexpressible. But when we reached the summit of the first range our bodies seemed endowed with an excess of agile strength, and the expanded mind desired to dash at one falcon-sweep through the vast circumference of this wilderness of richest luxuriance and loftiest sublimity. We recognised from here the Fort of Ramghur on an apparently low ridge, and beyond rose the broad, snowy barrier of the Himalaya.

A fatiguing, but very pleasant ride of six or seven miles brought us to our Bechoba, which was pitched at a water mill near the hamlet of Kotul. Those of our followers who had come from Gwalior and the Deccan, were excessively fatigued by this first trial of mountain roads, and upon descending to the cool clear stream at Kotul they ran headlong into it, and then stretched themselves on its swarded banks in seemingly an eternal repose.

It was a delightful spot. There was a seclusion from the world, a freshness in the verdure, a sparkling in the streamlet, a subdued wildness in the prospect. We were enjoying our breakfast, having picked some white raspberries, the first that we had seen, and were pouring out our thoughts upon the grandeur and loveliness of the Himalaya, when we were startled by a yell of despair, followed by horrible vociferations of "Sheytaun! Sheytaun!" and upon running out we perceived one of our fattest Hindoo servants, rushing he knew not where, with both his hands glued far back below his hips, and his long white lungootee, or waist-cloth, his only dress, streaming in most unwarrantable disarray between his legs. He bellowed "Sheytaun" again and again, till the dell rang.* As he appeared insane, we had him

* "Il y a, selon la doctrine des Musulmans, plusieurs sortes ou espèces de Démons. Les uns sont appellez Ginn et Péri, qui sont ceux que nous appellons les Esprits follets

entrapped, but he continued capering as if possessed by every demon in the nether sphere, nor would he move his hands from where he had fastened them. We could obtain no answer from him, and were at a loss to conceive the cause of this conduct, until one of his companions from the crowd which had collected upon hearing these elaborate cries, told us, that after bathing he had chosen a place among some bushes to sit down, where as if enchanted he had sprung up and began performing these many antics. He pointed to the spot which was close by, and we discovered that the hapless Hindoo had sat down in a clump of gigantic nettles. There was no cure for it but

---

et les Fées, les autres Tecouin, qui sont les Parques des Payens, qui président au destin des Hommes. Il y a de plus les Div, que quelques uns confondent avec les Géans, quoy qu'ils ne soient pas le l'espèce des hommes. Il y a encore les Goul et Afriet, qui sont les Méduses, les Empuses, les Furies, et les Spectres, des Mythologistes, et enfin le pire de tous est Scheïthan et les Schaïathin, Satan et les Satans, qui sont Lucifer et toute la Troupe infernale."—*D'Herbelot. Bibliotheque Orientale, ad vocem. A la Haye.* J. Neaulme, &c, 1778, 4to. 4 vols.

patience. However, as the poor man fancied that, according to the observances of his religion, he had by the unfolding of his lungootee rendered himself impure, he jumped into the water to perform his ablutions;* but alas! his stinging tortures were redoubled by the cold immersion, which he tried to relieve, by putting the muscles of his face and body into every possible contortion, and at the same time calling upon every Deity and Demi-god that he in the midst of his anguish could remember, to soothe the burning pain.

We remained here in order to refresh ourselves and followers, till 2 H. 30 M. P. M., and then mounting our horses once more, we soon ascended by a zig-zag road to Chumboo, which is on the crest of the ridge; its elevation is 5000 feet. From this point the view was more magnificent, than any we had seen before; for not only was the snowy chain of the Himala more distinct, but the intervening space also was more extensive. From here our descent lay through fine pine forests, and as the

* Institutes of Menu, c. 11. "On Penance and Expiation," v. 203.

day was warm, the rich odour peculiar to them was so densely diffused throughout, that it seemed to weigh upon the air, and almost thicken it into liquid perfume. We were likewise gratified with fine prospects of the Baree Daybee mountain, Soorujghur on the Malown range, and Semla and Subahtoo. The descent was 2100 feet, and brought us to a branch of the Gumbur which runs below Subahtoo. Crossing the stream and ascending the abrupt side of the mountain, 1300 feet, we reached the Goorka Cantonments at Subahtoo. Being unaccustomed to mountain travelling we were very much fatigued, but forgot all in the grandeur of Nature around us, and the kindness of Captain Kennedy and our enterprising friends the Gerards.

Subahtoo, the Head Quarters of one of our Goorka Battalions, is situated on a small table-land at an elevation of 4205 feet, surrounded by high mountains, such as Baree Daybee, 7003 feet, Semla distant twenty-three miles, 7400 feet, the Fort of Jungala, which is on a peak beyond the Sutluj, and distant between thirty and forty miles, at least 10,000 or 11,000 feet, and the Kurroll Peak 7612 feet. The Snowy Range, too, is almost always visible from here, and the climate now, is like that of our summer in England. Thus while our minds enjoy the ampleness of Nature's creation, our senses are soothed by the mildness of the season.

We stayed at Subahtoo till the 4th of May, making arrangements for our further progress, which was a business of the utmost importance. Our elephants, which to the utter amazement of the Goorkas, had been brought on with us here, were now sent back under the escort of the party of horse which had accompanied us from Gwalior. With them also went our own Arab horses. Many of our servants, and the Palankeens were to remain at Subahtoo, and instead of them, we procured Goonts, Mules, Chumpalas, Doolees, and Hill Porters. My future travelling establishment consisted of six mules, and sixty-one porters for my baggage; and my friend and fellow-traveller had not less.

CHAPTER III.

SUBAHTOO TO KOTEGHUR.

5th May, *Syree,* 12m. 2f., elevation 4971 feet.—We left Subahtoo at 4 P.M. and descended to Deontul, a small hamlet on the main branch of the Gumbur river. It is about 1400 feet below the Cantonments, and 3m. 4f. distant by the road from them. The immediate descent into this narrow and romantic glen was very steep. The peasantry of the neighbourhood were reaping the corn with the sickle, as in England, and carrying away the produce in Kiltees or baskets of a conical form slung over the shoulders upon the back, as from the precipitous nature of the flanks of the hills upon which the terraced fields are made, they are precluded from the possibility of any other mode of conveyance. From hence we began ascending along the bank of the river, and passing the Fort of Hurreepoor which belongs to the Rajah of Putteeala, Mumleeg, and the Sohur Temple, reached Syree at nightfall, where there is a comfortable house built by Government for the accommodation of travellers. All our wants in the shape of provisions were supplied from a Bunneea's shop.

We shot several Chuckore, a large kind of partridge, in the fields below the house.* Our ascent from Deontul has been considerable, about 2100 feet, but it was generally gradual, and as the route was excellent, we rode without any inconvenience.

6th May, *Semla,* 10m. 4f., elevation 7400 feet.—The mountain air seemed to have instilled ether into my veins, for I felt as if I could have bounded headlong down into the deepest glens, or sprung nimbly up their abrupt sides with a daring ease. I therefore walked the whole of the way from choice. About three miles from Syree we came

* Perdix Chukor.

to Jantee Daybee, a temple containing numerous rude images, and surrounded by cherry-trees bending with fruit. Two miles more brought us to the Gumbur, which we crossed, and then began a very long ascent, which continued to Semla. A great portion of the ether in my blood evaporated during this part of the route. However, I cannot say that I was fatigued, for towards the end of the march, the road lay through a noble wood of cedars, pines, and oaks, and large Rhododendron-trees glowing with bunches of rich scarlet blossoms.* The prospects too had been magnificent, but upon reaching the crest of the ridge at Semla, the vastness of the scene became oppressive. The lofty snowy range shone from the dense azure of the heavens. Its giant flanks were broken with black mural precipices, and profound ravines, which were purple from their depth. Below was heaped a shattered mass of mountains, peaks and glens, ridges and valleys, some aridly bare, others luxuriantly rich. The ready materials for another world.

* Rhododendron Arboreum.

This day's journey I shall always remember, for it reminded me of home, the days of my boyhood, my mother, and the happiest of varied recollections. It was not, however, the effect of the prospects, for they were unlike those amongst the Welsh hills, but it was because I recognised a great number of trees and flowers common there; such as the fir, the oak, the apricot, the pear, the cherry, together with wild roses, raspberries, strawberries, thistles, dandelions, nettles, daisies, and many others. There was, too, an indescribable something in the breeze, which brought back a comparative similarity of feelings. I shall never forget this day.

The ascent between Syree and Semla was very great, but the road was broad and excellent, though leading over and along the sides of high mountains. The enormous valleys and dells, although they were precipitous descents of 1000 and 2000 feet were occasionally well cultivated, and also abundantly irrigated by streamlets frequently conducted from remote springs. Many of the mountains around Semla, which are the mere vassals of the mighty

Himala, would be the boast of other countries, as Wartoo or Huttoo 10,673 feet, Jungala between 10,000 and 11,000 feet, the larger Shallee 9623 feet, the Choor Pahar 12,149 feet, and Jukkoo 8120 feet. Over these the Snowy Range extends from N. 30° W. to N. 70° E., embracing consequently an angle of 100 degrees. The general appearance of this mass of snow is that of a wide undulating plain from which peaks rise in every imaginable shape. Their general height is from 16,203 to 25,749 feet,* from 1000 to 10,000 feet of which is covered with eternal whiteness, the disputed line of perpetual snow on the Southern side of this first high chain, being 15,000 feet. Between these peaks are the Passes which lead into Koonawr and Chinese Tartary, the principal of which are those nearest to us, as the Shatool 15,555 feet, the Yoosoo 15,877 feet, and the Boorendo 15,171 feet. This first barrier however is but the screen to other assemblages of higher mountains, which again are still the

* Asiatic Researches, vol. 14, p. 324, et seq.

inferiors of the world-like bulwarks on the left bank of the Indus, from whence they slope to the Steppes of Tartary and are at length lost in the immeasurable deserts of Cobi, and the deep woods and countless marshes of Siberia. The summits of this highest range have been estimated upon good grounds by my most adventurous and intelligent friends, J. G. Gerard, and A. Gerard, who alone have explored many portions of these wild recesses, to rise to the enormous elevation of 30,000 feet. Within these towering bounds, the general appearance of the region is mournful and barren. There, surrounded by the most gigantic pinnacles of the universe, Sublimity sits fettered to Desolation. It awes the mind!

Upon looking in an opposite direction to the Himala, the verge of sight is bounded by the Punjaub and the plains around Sirhind. We perceive the Sutluj winding along till lost in the glowing distance. Dark lines and spots mark the towns and villages, and the luridly glaring air over them indicates a burning wind, which can never reach this happy mountain region. We could see Subahtoo on an arid spot below us. Almost level with us are the summits of the Baree Daybee and Kurroll mountains, while beneath, the lower hills spread out in every direction, in the confusion even of irregularity. The spot we are upon is a ridge with deep valleys on either side filled with dark woods where it is impossible to cultivate the soil; but wherever the ground admits of husbandry, the usual successive lines of terraces appear covered with corn, and dotted with hamlets and houses, the roofs of which are as we can see by the glass, of slate. Their general look is that of neatness and comfort. Their inhabitants, undisturbed by the traveller, are shut out from the world. In many places, the terraced-fields are carried up to an extraordinary height, and there the effects of increasing elevation upon the temperature of the atmosphere are strikingly observable from the diversity of tints the produce assumes. The highest is in fresh blade and brilliantly green, while the lowest is sere and ripe. Close on the east the mountain Jukkoo rises 700 or 800 feet above our tents, from the summit of which the vast prospect is yet more vast. Jukkoo is mantled with hoary cedars, oaks clustered with acorns, and Rhododendron-trees blushing with bloom.*

We walked out in the evening upon the road leading to Koteghur. It is shaded by trees of the most elegant forms and varied foliage. The air too was cool, indeed sharp, and consequently to us who had borne the burning heats of the Deccan,

* The Deodar, or Kelon of the Hills, Pinus or Cedrus Deodara, figured by Mr. Lambert at Tab. 52 of the 8vo. edition of his work on the Coniferæ, is, however, the most celebrated, and the longest known Himalayan species; having been noticed even by Avicenna (deiudar of the Latin translation): "est ex genere abhel (juniperus) que dicitur pinus Inda; et Syr. diudar est ejus lac." The Deodar is found in Nepal, Kemaon, and as far as Cashmere, and at elevations of from 7000 to 12,000 feet in Sirmore and Gurhwal, as on Manma, Deobun, Choor, Kedarkanta, and Nagkanda."—*Royle's Illustrations of the Bot. Himalayan Mountains*, p. 350.

The species of the genus Quercus are numerous in the Himala. Ten are described in *Don's Prod. Flor. Nepalensis*, p. 56, et seq., 1 vol. 8vo. London, Gale, 1825.

4. Rhododendrum arboreum, Sm. * * * * Arbor 20 pedalis, v. ultra, sempervirens, ramosissima, tempore florendi speciosissima. * * * Flores terminales numerosi, densè corymbosi.—*Don's Prod. Flor. Nepal.* p. 154.

delightful. Around us also grew hollies, wild mint, ferns, and many other plants of a northern climate. It was Europe not Asia. To complete our joy, when we returned at night we were obliged to light a fire!

7th May, *Semla.*—One of the most magnificent sights in these mountains is to see the sunrise from some high peak, and we had therefore resolved last night to avail ourselves of the first opportunity to witness it by ascending to the summit of Jukkoo before daybreak. We were, however, disappointed, for upon reaching the top, the sun had already risen. To the East the Himala was almost hid in the blaze of light. We saw nevertheless what we considered the two Jumnootree peaks. They bore nearly due East, and though estimated to be eighty miles distant, they towered high above the snowy wilderness around them. The Choor Pahar seemed very near to us, and almost upon a level with our station. Ramghur was likewise visible, and beyond, the Sutluj glittered like a vein of silver on the distant plains. The summits of

Kurroll, Wartoo, and Barree Daybee, appeared beneath us.

In order to approximate by the simple means of the compass which I had with me, the length and direction of the Snowy Range, I took the bearings from Captain Herbert's Observatory, of the two extreme points as seen from it, which were as follows:—

Jumnootree or a lofty Peak near it. . N. 86° E.

Peak at the Western extreme. . . . . . N. 30° W.

consequently as Jumnootree is known to be eighty miles distant, and the Western extreme is estimated at ninety miles, the extent of this range of unfading snows visible from here is 145 miles, running from N. 60° W. to S. 60° E.

Thermometer: lowest 56°, highest 71°.5, Fahrenheit.

8th May, *Semla.*—We reached the summit of Jukkoo long before daybreak, and anxiously awaited the dawn. The sky appeared an enormous dome of the richest massy sapphire, overhanging the lofty pinnacles of the Himalaya, which were of indescribably deep hues, and strangely fantastic forms. At length five vast beaming shadows sprung upwards from five high peaks, as though the giant day had grasped the mighty barrier to raise himself, while in the same instant the light rolled in dense dazzling volumes through the broad snowy valleys between them, and soon the glorious orb arose with blinding splendour over the Yoosoo Pass, and assumed the appearance of a god-like eye! In a moment these rising solitudes flung off their nightly garments of the purest blue, and stood arrayed in robes of glowing white. The intermediate mountains cast their disjointed dark broad shadows across the swelling ranges below, the interminable plains were illumined, all the gorgeous, all the ineffable variety of earth became distinct; it was day, and the voiceless soul of the great globe seemed to rejoice smiling!

9th May, *Mahhasoo*, 9 m., elevation 9078 feet.—The road to-day was as usual along ridges, and the flanks of mountains. The dells beneath were very deep. It was fortunately broad, otherwise the march would have been dangerous. We were astonished to see the Goonts winding along the edges of precipices where a stumble would have been death, and also how obstinately they persisted when climbing steep ascents, in stopping to regain breath and refresh themselves. Their instinct is wonderful, and it would be dangerous to interfere with their peculiar habits; the best plan is to allow them to do what they choose, and hold on fast. The best breed of Goonts is from Ladak in Chinese Tartary. I purchased one for 170 rupees (£17), and was well satisfied with my bargain, for he was a stout, thick-set, broad-backed fellow, and mathematically correct in his steps.

I walked the entire distance from choice, and although the ascents were extremely fatiguing, I forgot the labour in the magnificence of the scenery. The woods also that we passed through were large and stately, filled with towering cedars, and noble oaks. We remarked also a species of sycamore, and black currant bushes. On the route were neither inhabitants nor villages, though in the glens we descried many hamlets.

Mahhasoo is a small temple built of wood and stone, dedicated to Siva, and situated upon a peak above the road. The style of its architecture is Chinese, and as it is the first of the kind which we have seen, we have been very much pleased with it. Its elevation is 9078 feet, which is the highest point that we have yet attained. It is a lonely spot, there not being even a Bunneea's shop to supply the wants of our camp. On each side of the crest from whence the peak rises, are dells from 1500 to 2000 feet deep, filled with forests of the finest cedars, oaks, and other trees. We have been particularly struck with the enormous size of the cedars, many of which are from 13 to 15 feet in circumference, and from 120 to 140 feet high. Our tents are pitched upon a fine green sward, unbroken by rank grasses or underwood, which appears to have been tended with care, not by the hand of man, but that most perfect one of nature. It is enamelled with lovely flowers, and as it is sloping, has the appearance of a large and costly Persian carpet.

But that which engrosses our attention most, is the far-stretching Snowy Range, which, though the summits of Wartoo, the Choor Pahar, and Sirgool are all hooded in snow and appear on a level with us, nevertheless fascinates our eyes. We are now completely bosomed in the mountain region which extends from these peaks of everlasting snow, to the fevered plains of Sirhind, which we see from this lofty station, and whilst enjoying the refreshing breeze, pity those whom their heat enfeebles by its intensity. But let us turn to the Himala. The three mighty peaks of Jumnootree, bearing S. 88° E., shoot up from the snowy chain to an immense altitude. Two of them are connected by a ridge, the third is at some distance, isolated and black, contrasting singularly with the hoary desert around it. Their elevation respectively is 21,155 feet, 20,122 feet, and 20,916 feet. Other peaks which we presumed to be above the source of the Ganges are still further east, and on that side close the view. The Shatool, Yoosoo, and Boorendo Passes, though actually more than forty-five miles distant, appear close to us, such is the delicate purity of the atmosphere. Beyond this first barrier we see the sacred summit of Kailas or Raldung, a precipitous, black, triangular pyramid, scantly streaked with snow. Its height is 21,411 feet.

Thermometer yesterday: lowest 52°; highest 72°, Fahrenheit.

Thermometer to-day: lowest 56°.5; highest 66°, Fahrenheit.

10th May. *Bunnee Chowkee,* in the Purgunnah of *Fagoo,* 2 m. 2 f., elevation 8107 feet.—This morning the ground at Mahhasoo was covered with hoar frost, and as the sun had risen in splendour we remained till the afternoon in the hopes of enjoying once again the grandeur of the scene. But it became cloudy soon after sunrise, and the Snowy Chain was partially obscured: we therefore proceeded on our journey with regret. However, we should not regret, for it is impossible that Semla and its sublimity can ever be effaced from our minds. The road lay still through cedar forests, which made our walk very delightful. On our left was the great Shallee Peak, and between was a wide and deep glen which ran down to the dell of the Sutluj. It was tolerably well cultivated and wooded. The hamlets which we saw, with their pent-roofs of slate, had a neat appearance. After descending 1000 or 1100 feet we gradually ascended to Bunnee. On the roadside I found a primrose. It seemed to be the casket of all my early thoughts.* From our tents the Choor Pahar and Wartoo mountains are seen connected by an enormous barren ridge of great height from which gigantic spines stretch to the Girree river, which is 5000 feet below the spot we are upon, and distant five miles. The broad ravines thus formed are partially cultivated. One of them is called the Purgunnah of Bulsum. Beyond this connecting ridge rises the Sirgool, wooded and streaked with snow. It is higher than Wartoo, and next in magnitude to the Choor Pahar. Upon a hill just above us, is the old Fort of Daysoo, and below, a deep valley which runs down to the Girree river.

* Primula Stuartii? "We find P. Stuartii with its rich yellow glow."—*Royle's Illus. Bot. Himalaya Mountains*, p. 310.

There is no village at Bunnee; it is merely a good wooden house for the accommodation of travellers. We have quitted the Kaentul Purgunnah, and are in that of Fagoo. The Ranee of Kaentul lives at Junnuk,

Our party now consists of several friends from Subahtoo, and time passes in continued pleasure. Besides, the invigorating air of these mountains has almost restored to health my valued friend and companion Major Close, who already begins to enjoy, unharassed, the magnificence of the scenery, and to walk a considerable distance without fatigue.

I took the following bearings with my compass from Mahhasoo.

Highest Jumnootree Peak ....N. 86° 30′ E.
The space between the two
connected Peaks.............S. 88° E.
Sreekanta, near Gungootree ....S. 80° E.

Thermometer: lowest 48°, highest 63° Fahrenheit.

11th May, *Mutteeana,* 15 m. elevat. 8000 ft. At 5 o'clock, A. M., we started, and at 9 h. 30 m., A. M., reached the house here, a good deal tired.

The walk was nevertheless very agreeable. The road was excellent, leading generally along the summit of a bare ridge, though sometimes across the sides of the mountains. At 6 m. 4 f. we passed the Fort or Blockhouse of Tayog (Theog), formerly a Goorka Post. A hill State takes its name from this Fort. The elevation of Tayog is 8018 feet. Between it and Mutteeana there are two Gauts, the Kunnaug and the Punta. The elevation of the former is 8409 feet, and of the latter 8500 feet. The Punta Pass divides Tayog from Komarsain, another hill State.

The ascent of the Kunnaug is long and somewhat laborious. We were particularly struck to-day by the depth of the glens, which varied from 3000 to 5000 feet, and again occasionally traversed fine woods of oak and fir. There were numerous hamlets in the dells. Their inhabitants are almost as much out of sight as if they dwelt in Kamschatka. The most prominent objects were, on the left, the Shallee Peak with its Temple dedicated to the Goddess Kalee, to whom formerly human sacrifices were offered, and on the right the towering mass of the Sirgool,* I loitered away half an hour in shooting, but only killed a chukore. I fired also at a jackal, the first wild quadruped which I have seen since entering the mountains. There are but few animals to be met with near the side of the road. We have seen eagles, white vultures, crows, maïnas, tom-tits, hawks, cuckoos, chukores, pheasants, sparrows, and some other small birds, the names of which I could not ascertain, but of those which I have enumerated the number is small. Some of our party saw some kukkurs, a species of deer. A large lizard, like a gosamp, was killed by the camp people.

* The name of the black goddess, to whom these human sacrifices were offered, was Nareda, or Callee, who is exhibited in the Indian temples sacred to her worship, with a collar, not composed, like that of the benign deities, of a splendid assemblage of the richest gems, but of golden skulls, descriptive of the gloomy rites in which she took so gloomy a delight. "To her," says Sir W. Jones, "human sacrifices were anciently offered as the Vedas enjoined, but, in the present age, they are absolutely prohibited, as are also the sacrifices of bulls and horses."

Maurice's Indian Antiquities, Dissert. 2, p 181.*

Jumnootree and the Snowy Chain were visible for some miles along our march, but here we are surrounded by lofty mountains which confine the view to within moderate bounds. Mutteeana is situated on a high ridge overlooking a deep glen to the westward, and the steepness of its sides may be conceived from the circumstance of our amusing ourselves, a frequent pastime amongst the inhabitants of this country, in rolling down large stones, which slided slowly at first, then sprung heavily from spot to spot, and suddenly increasing their velocity bounded far and lightly, surmounting many of the trees in their way, and even when we had lost sight of their long whirling leaps, we could still hear the echoes of their successive heavy footings in the profound depths below. How full is nature of moral similes! To what a thousand different comparisons of vicious careers might this be applied? How sacred are the pages of this volume! Alas! how seldom read!

Thermometer: lowest 53°.5. Highest 66° Fahrenheit.

11*th May*, Naugkunda, 11 m. elevation 9016

feet.—This has been the most fatiguing walk I ever took. I went by the old road, and began with a descent of 1600 feet to the Kuljur river, which is a branch of the Girree, from whence a steep ascent of 1200 feet brought me to the crest of the mountain. At 3 m. 4 f. I reached Maandunnee, where there are two temples, which are very well worth visiting, chiefly as specimens of the ingenuity of the mountaineers.

The smaller, which is about 30 feet high, is of an oblong form, built of stone and wood, and covered with a pent-roof. A figure of Gunnais, carved in wood, is over the entrance, which is also decorated with the antlers of deer, small circular pieces of iron and brass, little flags, or rather shreds of cloth, and many other reliques, the offerings of pilgrims.

The larger temple is consecrated to Daybee. It is entirely of wood, elaborately carved, and stands upon a square stone terrace. The roof is pyramidal, surmounted by a wooden umbrella, from the edge of which small elegantly wrought pieces of wood are suspended, which, being moved by the wind, strike against each other, and produce a simple but agreeable sound. The interior of the temple is also richly carved into figures of Hindoo deities. Maandunnee is inhabited entirely by Brahmins. Its elevation is 7428 feet. A long walk from here brought me to a nullah, above which the Naugkunda Gaut rose 1700 feet. The ascent, from its abruptness and the excessive heat, was very laborious, but I got over it with pleasure, for the road passed through woods of cedar and oak, was crossed frequently by rills of the purest water, and deliciously refreshing, and the views from many points were magnificent. To the right Wartoo rose to a prodigious height in massive grandeur from the dell beneath, with its head besprinkled with snow, and its flank mantled with corn and forest. Its peak is surmounted with a ruinous fort, which looks like a gray falcon cowering on its nest. Before me the Naugkunda ridge, which sweeps from Wartoo to the left, added to the grandeur of the prospect. It was also clothed with forests, and the road running over it, cut into numerous zig-zags, showed curiously. The Hill-porters, mules, goonts, my friends and our attendants, climbing up it, were diminished to points, and appeared to hang over me. When I reached the summit the Snowy Chain burst suddenly upon my view, in all its huge, yet aërial sublimity. There was a good deal of cultivated ground on each side of the road to day.

There is an excellent Bungala on this gaut for travellers. We shall, to-morrow, quit the pioneer road, which ends at Koteghur, in order to make an excursion to Wartoo.

Thermometer lowest 53° highest 61° Fahrenheit.

13*th May*, Wartoo or Huttoo Fort, 3 m. 4 f, elevation 10,673 feet.—Our walk was delightful, except one portion immediately after leaving Naugkunda, when we had to wind along the side of a frightful precipice with the path little more than a foot wide, and the dell 1700 feet deep beneath. It was so bare and steep that a false step would have been fatal. The Hill porters, however, who carried the chumpalas, made light of it, though I felt the utmost anxiety for my son, who was in one of them. Passing this dangerous place it was perfectly safe and agreeable, running along one of the enormous gnarled ridges of Huttoo, and overshadowed by a thick forest of cedar, pine and oak. The steep ascent was directly below the Fort, and it was difficult, as the route lay amongst shattered rocks, and over beds of snow. Immediately we reached the first patch of snow we pelted each other, to the great amusement of our servants, and particularly my son. He walked almost the whole way, and when, towards the end, he became tired, the good-natured Hill-porters carried him upon their backs.

We saw, to-day, the first yew and walnut trees, as well as hazel bushes, or rather I should say trees, for they are of very large growth here.*

* Taxus baccata? The yew.

Juglans regia. "Walnuts are imported into the plains of India from the Himalayas, but chiefly from Cashmere. They are known to the Arabs by the name of jouz, or the nut. The Hindoos call them ukhrot, and the Persians chuhar mughz (four brains.")—*Royle's Illust. Bot. Himal. Mountains*, p. 342.

After the tents were pitched, and we were refreshed, we amused ourselves by making an immense snow-ball, near the brink of a very steep declivity, from whence, a few years before, a large bed of snow had slipped, and buried beneath its weight several of the country people, who were travelling that way. We had passed the spot on the road, which was marked by heaps of stones. When all was ready, we applied our united force to this mimic avalanche, which rushed crashing through the bushes, into the depths below. Our servants from the plains, who had never seen snow before, looked at it with that indifference which is so peculiar a mark of the Hindoo character.

Wartoo, like Jukkoo, is one of the lofty stations which was selected by Captain Hodgson and Lieutenant Herbert for prosecuting their great Trigonometrical operations, in order to determine

---

" Corylus extends from Cashmere to Kemaon, and is found in shady forests on the shoulders of such mountains as Choor and Kedarkanta; with the same species, C. lacera, on all."—*Ibid.* p. 343.

the heights of the snowy peaks of the Himalayan Chain. The Fort is now in ruins, but it was formerly occupied by the Goorkas. It is 1600 feet above Naugkunda.

Thermometer, lowest 41° highest 57° Fahrenheit.

14th May, *Wartoo.*—Yesterday evening there was a thunder-storm accompanied with hail. It was fearfully sublime. The huge clouds girdled with lightning rolled amongst the mountains, and the thunder burst so frequently, that it seemed almost to crack the firmament, while the wind hurried whistling through the gloomy woods. The vapoury masses then lowered into the valleys beneath, and hid them from us, and the snowy Himalaya was all that we saw. Between was a surging ocean of clouds, through which rugged peaks arose, like enormous breakers. As the tempest passed, height after height towered majestically, glowing with the crimson sun-flood of the evening, and threw their large purpled shadows far and wide upon the dispersing clouds, and the dismembered ridges which peered above them. All became at last distinct, and the air was still. During the night it again rained, and the wind was heavy, but it cleared up before daybreak.

The summit of Wartoo is covered with charming woods, and a sward diapered with the most beautiful flowers. It were impossible to be fatigued by wandering here. On all sides grow the yellow buttercup and one, also, of a lilac colour, the strawberry is flowering; and a crowd of wildings besides rear their graceful forms, and nod in the gentle breeze.* In the woods we saw several pheasants, and for the first time for many years, heard the throstle discoursing most excellent music. Indeed, this day we admired Nature in all her loveliness and sublimity. Before us rose the lofty and infinite realm of eternal snow, the Himalaya. On its eastern bounds Jumnootree, Jaunlai, and another peak stood like giants mantled in white, gazing at the intense

* Ranunculus arvensis? The buttercup.

Anemone discolor. *Royle's Illust. Bot. Himal. M.* p. 52.

Fragaria vesca. Wild strawberry.

azure firmament above. To the west a group of their equals were assembled, wrapped also as in profound contemplation of the heavens. The glistening plain on which they stood, was broken by black precipitous rocks, and broad, steep beds of spotless snow, and intervening were rugged cliffs, wooded heights, cultivated ravines, temples and villages, a disjointed mountain realm — Oh! the feebleness of language! the fulness of the heart! a teardrop is the only eloquence! We bowed to our mother Nature in respect.

15th May, *Koteghur*, 8 m. elevat. 6634 ft. It was with great regret that we quitted Wartoo. The pathway which we followed was good, but very steep, as may easily be conceived, from the descent being 4000 feet in 8 miles. The woods we passed through were very fine, and their shelter delightful. The Sutluj is 4000 feet below Koteghur, and 5 miles distant. Such is the gigantic scale of these regions. I estimated the extent of the snowy range, as seen from Wartoo, running from N. W. to S. E., at 180 miles, the nearest point of which was that westward of the Shatool, Yoosoo, and Boorendo Passes. It was 25 miles from where we stood, but such was the ethereal transparency of the atmosphere, that it seemed within gunshot. Every rock and fragment lying upon the snow, nay every rent in the snow was distinct. Indeed I think that if it were possible for a man on horseback to be there, they would be perfectly visible.

Upon our arrival at Koteghur we were kindly greeted by my friend Captain Patrick Gerard, who is in command of a portion of the Goorka Battalion, which is stationed at this remote point. He employs his leisure hours in scientific observations on the meteorology of these elevated countries, as well as in making collections of plants and minerals. His brothers, Captain Alex. Gerard, and Surgeon James Gerard, together with Lieut. Osborne, now form our delightful party.

Thermometer at Wartoo: lowest 42°.5.

Thermometer at Koteghur: 75° Fahrenheit.

16th May, *Koteghur*. We were visited to-day

by the son of the Rajah of Komarsain, a handsome boy, ten years old, who is a great and deserved favourite of Captain P. Gerard. He came almost unattended. He is of a fair complexion, with mild Hindoo features, and has a natural nobility of manner which is most engaging; had it not been for this, his simple dress of Sooklaat and flat black woollen cap, round which he had put some wild flowers gathered on his way, would scarcely have distinguished him from the peasantry. The object of his visit was to invite us to Komarsain. He presented us with flowers, which is the customary compliment in this country, and soon formed an acquaintance with my son, in whom he found a joyful playmate.

21st May, *Koteghur*, We have now been long enough at Koteghur to form nearly a just estimation of all that it offers, and I have no hesitation in saying, that, if society could be obtained, it is the place where I should desire to pass the remainder of my life. Its climate is temperate, its sky deep yet brilliantly blue, and its surrounding country full of majesty and sublimity. All these give a joyousness to the mind, and health to the body. More cannot be asked, nor can more be found. It is only at this elevation, and in this parallel of latitude that it exists.

Koteghur is situated in lat. 31° 19′ N. and long. 77° 30′ E. It is upon a slope of the Wartoo mountain. The Rauj of Komarsain lies to the westward of Koteghur, and is separated from it by a ravine between 3000 and 4000 feet in depth. Enormous mountains rise on both sides of the Sutluj and confine it to a narrow glen, through which it runs in a large body, with great rapidity. On the right bank of this river, northward and westward, are the states of Kooloo, Sookaid, and Mundee, one confused mountainous mass, whose elevation varies from 10,000 to 12,000 feet, and almost entirely obstructs the view of the Snowy Himala, a small portion only of which is seen, bearing from N. 8° E. to N. 28° E. The broad flanks and the curious flat summits of some of the mountains, wherever there is sufficient soil, are cultivated with an industry which is almost incredible The fields on the slopes are, as I have already mentioned, long, narrow strips of ground, which rise one above another like terraces to great elevations, even upon very steep declivities. The supporting wall of each is two, three, four, five, or six feet in height, according to the abruptness of the place. They are levelled with great care, and are watered by rills conducted sometimes from a considerable distance. They generally run from the highest, and overflow every part successively to the lowest. The effect of aspect and elevation upon the cultivation is very remarkable, for while on the uplands the produce is green, it has been reaped and carried at the base of the valley. Indeed this is extraordinarily exemplified in two gardens which Captain P. Gerard has at Koteghur, one of which is near the house where he resides, and the other in the dell, 4000 feet below. In the lower one plantains and other tropical fruits are abundant, while in the upper English fruits are equally plentiful.

The Hamlets are seldom of more than ten or fifteen houses, generally not so many. Single houses are numerous, and from their being scattered amongst the fields give an agreeable variety to the bold landscape. In those districts which border the plains, the dwellings, which are mere huts, have flat roofs; but here, where snow always falls in winter, the roofs made either of cedar also called Deodar, or of slates, are pent. They are of two or three stories, the lowest of which is invariably used for cattle, and when there are three, the second for grain, and the third, occupied by the family, is surrounded by a covered gallery, in which its inhabitants are generally seen sitting when at leisure. All the temples, and many also of the larger houses, have roofs after the Chinese fashion, which gives them a singular and pleasing appearance. The pitch of these roofs is very great, being formed by the disposition of planks into two concave curves, joined at the summit, and diverging down to the walls, where they project horizontally three or four feet into eaves. The walls are of wood or stone, sometimes both, and the buildings are very substantial.

The natives of this country are not so fair as I had expected. The men are not unfrequently tall, all of them strong, but few of them handsome. Many of the women are pretty. The dress of both sexes is nearly the same. It always consists of a drab coloured shirt and frock of woollen cloth, called Sooklaat, trousers of the same material, and, in this district, a flat black woollen cap. They also all bind a girdle round the waist. The women, instead of the cap, wear a piece of cloth about the head, and twist their hair into one immense long plait, the end of which is ornamented with slips of coloured cloth, and reaches to the ground. As, however, few can boast of so great a length of natural hair, vanity, the real mother of all arts, has taught them to make up the deficiency with wool. They are also very fond of ornaments, their arms and ankles being covered with armlets and anklets, to as great an extent as means are compatible with wishes. These are of various materials, as silver, brass, iron and polished bone. They also, like the Hindoostanee women, wear the Nut'h.* The plait is very becoming, strange as it may appear at first sight, but only, to tell the truth, in young women; so true it is that any dress adorns the beauty of youth. All agricultural labours, with the exception of ploughing, are done by the females, while the men too commonly sit idling at home; but such, indeed, is the state of the sex in all uncivilized communities. The corn, as we have seen, is cut with the sickle, and is carried away by the women, in Kiltees, or large baskets, slung over the shoulders, the general mode of bearing burdens in the mountains. A man will often carry one hundred pounds weight in this manner for ten or twelve miles, over rugged and steep roads, or rather paths, which, to a stranger, are difficult enough without any load.

An extraordinary custom is prevalent amongst

* The Nut'h is a ring of gold, or other metal, sometimes ornamented with precious stones, and varying in size, which is worn hanging from the cartilage of the nose, as an ear-ring from the ear. " The rings, and nose jewels."—*Isaiah* ch. iii. ver. 21.

these mountaineers, the origin of which it would be very difficult to trace. Like the Nairs, on the Malabar coast, it is usual for a woman to have three, four, and even five husbands.* We know that, formerly, female infanticide was of general occurrence here, and even under the Goorka rule, they sold their daughters to the

* "In the Tohuffat ul Mujahed it is written, that the husbandmen of Malabar are mostly infidels, and that their soldiers are called Nairs. The conjugal contract of the Nairs is performed by a string round the neck, and the wife may afterwards connect herself with whatever other men she pleases. Thus one woman, without a formal contract, may have several husbands, with whom she may repeatedly associate at nights by rotation. Carpenters, smiths, and dyers, who are not Brahmans, follow this practice as well as the Nairs; and this was the custom of the infidel Gickers, in Panjab; for, before their conversion to the Mussulman religion, every woman used to have several husbands; and whenever any of the husbands visited her he used to leave his mark at the door, that, in case one of the others in the mean time should come, he might, upon seeing the mark, retire. And whenever a daughter was born, it was the custom to carry her out immediately, and call aloud to know who wanted her. If any one should express a desire to have her they gave her to him, and, if not, they killed her in an instant."—*Asiatic Ann. Reg.* 1799. *Misc. Tracts*, p. 156,

inhabitants of the plains for slaves. Can the custom, perhaps, be referrible to these causes?

The chief riches of the population consist in a few goonts, some horned cattle of a small breed, and goats and sheep. They have, too, a fierce race of dogs. The best Goonts are from Ladak, on the banks of the Indus, but they are likewise bred in Kooloo, Mundee, and other districts on the opposite side of the Sutluj.

The East India Company's small commercial establishment, at Koteghur, for the shawl wool, is merely experimental, being intended to turn the trade in this article from Cashmere to our own territories. The principal mart for shawl wool is Garoo, or Gartope, in Chinese Tartary, from whence it is now brought direct to Koteghur, through Koonawr, a district lying within the snowy mountains, and dependent upon the State of Bussheer. Two pounds weight of the picked wool costs, upon its arrival here, 8 or 9 rupees, or sixteen to eighteen shillings, and this quantity is sufficient to make a shawl. It is packed here and sent to England to be manufactured. This material is the produce of a species of goat, and is found under the hair of the animal. It is however but at Ladak and along the banks of the Indus as far as Garoo and the Lake Manasarowara, that this goat thrives, and its wool is the only staple commodity which the Company is desirous to obtain from those countries. Chowries or Yaks' tails,* which are used as fans, and musk, are also brought as staple articles from thence. In return the Company barters copper, steel, chintzes, and woollens, but hitherto only in small quantities.

Bussheer, in which Koteghur is situated, is one of the most extensive mountain States dependent upon our Government. Its capital, Rampoor, upon the Sutluj, is distant in a north-easterly direction from here twenty-one miles. The country surrounding Koteghur is a scene of grandeur. Looking down to the Sutluj which rolls 4000 feet below, we perceive broken ridges, pine forests, and numerous hamlets dispersed amongst masses of variegated cultivation, all diminishing gradually into the profoundly dis-

* Bos Grunniens. The Yak.

tant depths of the ravine. Raising the eye from thence, a towering object fills the sight. This is the mountain Jinjalla, crowned with a fort. Its elevation is 8000 feet. To the right of Jinjalla another mountain is seen, still higher and streaked with snow. There are besides around it, Sirinuggur, Ruggopoor, Buggora, Mungaroo, Chooassee, and many other peaks rising out of the dense clump of mountains before us, topped with forts. The most charming object of this picture is the cultivation, which flutters like a shaded pall of green upon the abrupt and swelling flanks of the enormous glens and valleys. To complete the majesty of the scene, a small portion of the vividly snowy Himalaya peers above the huge and tangled mountain screen.

Bearings from Koteghur per Theodolite.

Name.	Description.	District.	Bearing.
Sirinuggur....	Fort	Kooloo	333° 20′
Ruggopoor....	ditto	ditto	329° 50′
Buggora......	ditto	Mundee	315° 0′
Mungaroo	ditto	ditto	306° 25′

Name.	Description.	District.	Bearing.	
Chooassee	ditto	Sookaid	304°	5′
Jinjalla	ditto	ditto	299°	10′
Komarsain	Town	Komarsain	276°	45′
Nonoo Kunda..	Peak	Kooloo	0°	45′
Snowy Range			8° to 28°	

Diary of the Thermometer.

	Lowest.	Fahr.	Highest.
May 16th..........	57°	—	76°
„ 17th..........	57°	—	78°
„ 18th..........	55°	—	80°
„ 19th..........	56°	—	81°
„ 20th..........	57°	—	81°
„ 21st..........	59°	—	80°

CHAPTER IV.

FROM KOTEGHUR TO SOORAAN, THE SUMMER RESIDENCE OF THE RAJAH OF BUSSHEER.

22nd May, *Dutnuggur*, 12m., elevat. 3200 ft.—This has been a most fatiguing day. We left Koteghur at 4 P. M. on our goonts, and after a ride of three miles along a winding road through corn-fields, reached the summit of the descent to the Sutluj, which is 4000 ft. below. Here we dismounted and sent away our ponies, as they cannot go down by this path, but we expected to find our horses, which we had ordered yesterday to proceed by Komarsain and Keipoo, at the bottom. Looking at the Sutluj from the top of this descent, it semed little better than a muddy stream which might easily be jumped over, and a large village on its right bank, in Kooloo, appeared a small speck. A very steep, rugged, crooked pathway, leading at times over terraced fields, brought us in an hour and a quarter to the bed of the river. The distance was 2 m. 4 f. to 3 m., and the descent 4000 ft., which will give some idea of its abruptness and the shaking we got. Long before we reached the bottom, the increasing roars of the water made us think differently of the Sutluj, and when we stood upon its banks we were astonished at the rapidity with which it hurled itself through the high ravine, throwing surges upon the shore like the rising tide. From this spot, we saw, through an opening in the barrier of mountains, a small portion of the snowy chain which overlooked us, from a height of 13,000 ft. above where we stood, an object fit for contemplation.

By some mistake, our horses had proceeded to Dutnuggur, and we were consequently obliged to push forwards on foot. We crossed the Beearee torrent by a good sango, which is the usual kind of bridge in these mountains. They are merely two or three pine-trees, covered with chips and branches, thrown over a stream. From hence, we continued our walk to Nirt, a considerable village on the Sutluj, distant 8 m. 4 f. from Koteghur. Its elevation is 3087 ft. By this time, night had closed in, and we could scarcely find the road, while the thundering of the river rendered the gloom fearful. We next crossed the Muchar torrent also by a sango, but whether it was a good one or not, we could not see. Shortly after, we were rejoiced at perceiving the lights of our camp-followers' fires. It was 9 P. M. when we came to Dutnuggur, very much tired, too much so to scold our horse-keepers, and when we had supped, we were in too good a humour to attempt it.

Dutnuggur, is a large village on the Sutluj. It is in the midst of cultivation, the first which we have seen since quitting the foot of the Gaut below Koteghur.

23rd May, *Rampoor*, 8m. 4f., elevat. 3398 ft.—Upon leaving Dutnuggur, we travelled along a cultivated flat for two miles. Such an extensive piece of level ground is a curiosity in this precipitous country. Soon after, we crossed the Nowgurree torrent by an excellent sango. The stream is clear and rapid, and comes from the Snowy

Range, which we see up its course. It is twenty or twenty-five miles distant. This torrent joins the Sutluj on our left, a few yards from the road. The descent of the Sutluj, a short distance above its junction with the Nowgurree, is greater than usual, and the confused sounds and impatient tumult of its curved and fretted waves bounding over the rocks magnificent. Near here, are several large caves in the rock forming the flank of the mountain on the right, in which the sheep and goats that are brought here to graze are penned up at night. Four miles more brought us to Rampoor.

We found that the Rajah had proceeded to his summer residence at Sooraan, but by his special orders, his officers showed every attention to our wants and comforts. We were not sorry for his absence, as the heat was excessive, and in such weather, visits of ceremony are never agreeable. We did not pitch our Bechobas, but were accommodated with a house, built chiefly of wood, which belonged to the Rajah, and commanded a view of so strange an assemblage of objects, as always raised fresh curiosity. The town appeared nearly empty, from the Court having removed to Sooraan. This is the largest place we have seen since leaving the plains. It is the capital of Bussheer, an extensive and very mountainous State, containing districts on both sides of the Himalaya. The latitude of Rampoor is 31° 27′ N., longitude 77° 38′ E.

The glen of the Sutluj, at this season of the year, is insupportably hot; its width varying only from half a mile to a mile, while the mountains rise on either side of the river to elevations of 1500 to 3000 ft. Their sides are shattered and bare, and the scene though rude is noble. Here and there indeed, we perceive terraced fields, together with hamlets, perched upon points seemingly inaccessible.

The road from Koteghur here, with the exception of the descent to the Sutluj, which has not been made, is excellent. It runs along the course of the stream, and within a stone's throw of it, but sometimes rising above it two or three hundred feet. Rampoor is situated on the left bank, and contains about 150 houses, which are from one to three stories high, with roofs of thick slates. As it is the capital, some of the dwellings of the officers of state are of considerable size, roofed in the Chinese style.

The manufactures of the town are confined to Pusmeenas, and coarse cloths of the Beeangee wool. The Pusmeenas are shawls of an inferior quality, without a border, and when well dyed, are very beautiful. Dresses are made of them, which are light, warm, and very comfortable. The weight of one is about 2 lbs., and their value from 10 to 15 rupees, 1*l.* to 1*l.* 10*s.* each.

In May, October, and December, large fairs are held at Rampoor, which are frequented by inhabitants of the States beyond the Sutluj, as well as those from other parts of Bussheer, from Sirmoor, and some even from Ladak and Chinese Tartary.

There are three temples in the town dedicated to Seeta Ram, Nur Sing, and Salagram.* They are inconsiderable buildings.

* "It is not, however, only the conch-shell that is vene-

The object most deserving of attention at Rampoor is the Joola or rope bridge over the Sutluj. It is the first we have seen, and is a mode of crossing rivers, which seems to us both disagreeable and dangerous, except to sailors or mountaineers of these countries. They are, however, not of un-

---

rated by the Brahmins; there is a certain stone of a high mystical virtue, and for the same reason, consecrated to Veeshnu, called *salagram*, in which the Hindoos imagine they discover nine different shades, emblematical of his nine incarnations. It is found in the river of Casi, a branch of the Ganges, is very heavy, oval or circular in its form, and in colour it is sometimes black, sometimes violet. * * * * The Salagram is piously preserved in the temples of the Veeshnuvites, and is to them what the lingam is to the Seevites. The ceremonies performed to these stones are nearly similar; they are equally borne about, as somewhat superlatively precious, in the purest white linen; they are washed every morning, anointed with oils, perfumed, and solemnly placed on the altar during divine worship, and happy are those favoured devotees who can quaff the sanctified water in which either has been bathed."—*Maurice's Indian Ant.* vol. 5, p. 908, et seq.

"Nirsingh Owtar, was an animal, from the head to the waist, like a lion, and the lower parts resembling a man."—*Ayeen Akbery*, v. 2, p. 235.

Nirsingh, or Nrisingh, is an avatar or incarnation of Vishnu. He became incarnate under this form in order to frequent occurrence. This one is formed by two abutments of masonry on each side of the stream, each between twenty and thirty feet high. On the bank opposite to us, a strong upright beam is embedded in the buttress, and in the one on this side, two strong beams are laid horizontally and parallel with the current, the one nearest to the water being four feet above the other. Ten ropes, each about an inch in diameter, are bound to the upright beam on the bank opposite, passed over the highest horizontal beam here, and secured to the second, which is embedded in two low walls at right angles to the course of the river.

---

destroy Herenkisph, a Deyt, who had, by his austerities, so much pleased the Divinity, that power was given him to rule the earth and upper regions, and to be invulnerable to the attacks of all animals. He became impious through this beneficence, and was destroyed by Nirsingh.

Seeta Ram. Rama is another avatar of Vishnu. Seeta is his wife, who is a model of conjugal affection. Mr. Wilson has translated a beautiful play, "The Uttara Rama Cheritra," from the Sanskrit, which contains a great portion of their history. The fullest account, however, is in the Ramayana, translated by A. Schlegel and the Rev. Messrs. Carey and Marshman.

The length of these ropes is 211 feet, and they form, from not being tightly stretched, curves. A piece of wood, nearly two feet in length, hollowed like a trough, covers the ten ropes, and is made to traverse on them from one bank of the river to the other, by means of two ropes, which are pulled by a man on each side. From this trough, two ropes, made into a loop, are suspended, which is the seat for the passengers. Thus, in order to cross, a person sits in this loop, as a child in a swing, holds on with his hands, and is drawn over by the man opposite. Such is the usual make of the Joola.

The rushing and crushed waves of the rolling river, the noise of its waters, and its breadth, would have deterred us all, with the exception of Captain A. Gerard, who was accustomed to such traverses, from attempting, excepting under necessity, to pass over by the Joola.

On the right bank of the river in Kooloo, we see two forts, under an angle of 18° of elevation. The hypothenusal distance of each I estimated at about two miles, their height therefore above us is 3263 feet. A peak also in Kooloo, with an angle of elevation of 27°, whose hypothenusal distance I estimated at three miles, rises 7191 feet above the river. These are, however, but rude approximations. They remind me, nevertheless, accurately of the view. The snowy range is not visible from Rampoor.

Thermometer at 1 P. M. 102°, Fahrenheit.
2 P. M. 100° „ cloudy.
3 P. M. 76° „ storm, with rain and hail.

24th May, *Gowra*, 8 m. 4 f.—We left Rampoor at 5 A. M., and continued our route up the glen of the Sutluj, which was rugged and sterile, till we reached the village of Kunnair, 2 m. 4 f. distant from Rampoor. Half a mile further brought us to the hamlet of Jukkoo. Both these places were surrounded by cultivation. At a mile beyond this we stopped suddenly, in order to view at our leisure the first great obstacle to our further progress. This was the side of an excessively steep, bare mountain, over which the pathway was a seemingly perpetual zig-zag. However, we began to climb with great perseverance, as also did our attendants. One of them who carried a keg of herrings slung over his shoulder, when he had nearly reached the summit, by some inopportune chance, let it slip. Off it bounded like a truant, and the porter tried to run after the renegado, but vain was his attempt! We began to laugh, and turned to see the nursery ballad of "Jack and Gill" in performance. The place however was so abrupt, that the unfortunate man lost his footing, and to our horror, rolled headlong, for some distance, with the mercurial keg still far outstripping him. He however recovered himself, and stopped short. We were delighted; so was the keg, at this happy release from fear, for it went bounding in gracefullest curves, footing it lightly towards the Sutluj. Suddenly it burst, and the red-herrings shot upwards in exquisite irradiation, and then, as if taking a long farewell of earth, dropped silently into the roaring waters of the deep torrent, and pursued their liquid way to the Indus.

This ascent is a mile and a half in length by the road, and to those unaccustomed to such walks seems very dangerous, but it is more in appearance than reality. From hence the path ran for some distance evenly, with a frightful precipice almost overhanging the Sutluj, which rolled 1500 feet below on the left, and then turning the shoulder of the mountain, it passed through some pleasant woods of pine, and other trees, and by a small place called Shado, on to a fine stream, limpid as ether, which tumbled over rocks of quartz and hornblende; after crossing this we began to ascend the mural flank of a mountain by large rude steps, from which circumstance we called it Ladder-Hill, until we reached a wood, through which we descended gradually, and arrived at another streamlet, equally clear as the former, that rushed amongst masses of mica-slate. The banks of it were of a steatitic nature, glistening, and so very slippery, that we found it extremely difficult to climb the ascent opposite, which fortunately was not long. I was obliged to take off my shoes, and use both hands and feet to surmount the slope, which was very steep. From hence to Gowra our walk was through fields, in which we saw the wild apricot, the pear, the willow, nettles, butter-cups, and strawberries.*

Gowra is an agreeable spot on the flank of a ridge of the Himala, which juts into the Sutluj. The country in the vicinity is well tilled, and the views are fine. We see snow upon the mountains on either hand.

The Rajah of Rampoor has a small neat house here, close to which is a handsome temple, surrounded with an open trellis of wood. It is consecrated to Ruggonaut. We admired the carvings on it very much, and praised the taste, skill, and execution of the mountain artist.

We have just been visited by the Rajah of Bussheer, a handsome and vivacious boy of about thirteen. He was accompanied by his Wuzzeer Teekum Daas, and a small retinue. They were all clothed in woollen from head to foot, with the

* "The apricot is very abundant round almost every village in the Himalayas, rendering it difficult to ascertain whether it be ever found wild, as the trees remain the only vestiges of deserted villages."—*Royle's Illus. Bot. Himal. Mount.* p. 205.

exception of the Rajah, who was dressed in white linen, and wore a cap of gold brocade, with but few ornaments. We had heard that he was afflicted with goitre, but, though his neck was bare, we did not perceive any symptom of such a disease. He complimented Major Close upon his arrival into his mountain State, and not only proffered kindness, but acted with his meaning. Most of the persons with him wore garlands of flowers, or carried some in their hands. When they took leave they loaded us with them.

		Fahrenheit.	
Thermometer	at 1 P. M.	78°	
	at 2 P. M.	70°	rain
	at 3 P. M.	71°	cloudy
	at sun-set	66°	
	at sun-rise	58°	on 25th May.

25th May, *Mujjowlee*, 5 m. 4 f. elevation 5850 feet.—We passed by a good road, and surrounded by beautiful scenery, in succession, the villages of Daar 7 f., Bostal 1 m. 5 f., and Kurtoll 6 f. When, about a mile from Mujjowlee, we came to the crest of the hills overlooking the Munglaad valley and torrent. A little to the left, and at a profound depth in the glen, it joins the Sutluj. The mountains before us were covered with snow, and the aspect of the country was wild. We were now in the enormous embrasures of the Himalaya. On our route were many shady woods and rills of the purest water, gushing from the melting snows above. The profusion, too, of wild roses and other flowers, embalmed the air with exquisite fragrance. The rose was a creeper, and we frequently saw pines thirty feet high mantled in robes of the whitest blossoms, like so many maidens of the forest in their bridal garments. They were surpassingly graceful.*

Mujjowlee is a village of twenty or thirty houses. There is in it a temple dedicated to Lutchmee Narrain, before the entrance of which

* "Nothing can be more ornamental than the double white rose of Northern India, and the Deyra Doon, R. Lyellii, Kooza of the natives; nor than R. Brunonis, allied to R. moschata, Linn., common in the valleys, or the banks of streams within the mountains, ascending to the tops of lofty trees, especially alders, and hanging down in elegant racemes."—*Royle's Illust. Bot. Himal. Mount.* p. 203.

there is a rude figure of Nundee, and representations of some deities, which we could not distinguish.* It has a Chinese roof, and the doorways are ornamented with badly-carved figures of Gunnais and several other gods. Within upon a litter are seven brass busts of Lutchmee, Narrain, and others, which at stated times are carried in procession. These were presented by the Rajah of Bussheer.

The severity of the winters in this portion of the mountains, forces the inhabitants to bestow great care and expense upon their dwellings.

* "Sri, or Lakshmi, the goddess of beauty and abundance, at once the Ceres and the Alma Venus of India.

> Daughter of ocean and primeval night,
> Who fed with moonbeams dropping silent dew,
> And cradled in a wild wave dancing light.
>
> *Sir W. Jones's Ode to Lacshmi.*

Milman's Trans. Nala and Damayanti, note p. 120. Oxford, Talboys, 1 vol. 8vo., 1835.

"The Spirit of God, called Narayena, or Moving on the Water, has a multiplicity of other epithets in Sanscrit."—*Sir W. Jones's Hymn to Narayena*, vide Dissert. &c. on the History &c. of Asia, vol. 2, p. 352.

Nundee is the Bull "the vehicle of Siva, and the animal of the god is always painted of a milk-white colour."—*Wilson's Megha Duta*, note 113, p. 129. London, Black and Co., 1814, 1 vol. 8vo.

The women are handsome, and wear round flat caps like the men, but wind their hair round the head, and ornament it on each side behind the ears with large rosettes. Some of them dress in woollen trousers, others in large woollen wrappers which they put on in such fashion as makes the lower part form a petticoat. Both sexes, of every age, are passionately fond of flowers, and wear garlands of them suspended from their caps or round their necks.

The poppy is cultivated here to a considerable extent, as is ginger, for exportation. The Jerusalem artichoke is likewise grown. The oak is found wild in these elevated regions. Yesterday the Rajah sent us as a present an abundance of apples. The apricots are not yet ripe. The chief food of the inhabitants is wheat, barley, and rice, which are the prevailing grains.

This morning a Kholsa or hill-pheasant, and a bird resembling a magpie, were shot, and black partridges were heard calling in the fields.

As the sango over the torrent of the Munglaad had been represented to us as full of danger, and as it was on our to-morrow's route, I could not resist the curiosity of seeing it at once; and therefore, whilst our people were preparing the breakfast, I ran down into the glen and walked over it with ease. I then returned to my friends, to report that this time at least there was no difficulty to be apprehended.

Thermometer:	2 P. M. 86°	Fahrenheit.
"	3 P. M. 87°	"
"	4 P. M. 84°	"
"	sunset 76°	"
"	sunrise 64°	26th May

26th May, *Sooraan*, 6 m., elevation 7248 feet, lat. 31° 30′, N., long. 77° 46′ E.—Leaving our camp at 4 h. 50 m. A. M., we descended to the sango across the Munglaad torrent, which is 1100 feet below Mujjowlee. The path was upon an enormous slope of decomposing mica-slate, which where it was steep occasioned us some ludicrous slides. The sango is nothing more than two or three spars bound together by twigs and laid from rock to rock over the headlong stream. Upon these spars, some branches are placed so as to make a rude platform. It is only 15 feet in length, and 2 feet 6 inches or 3 feet in breadth, and two feet above the water. During the rains this is really a very dangerous passage, and many accidents have occurred, but to-day there was not the slightest hazard.

Immediately from here we toiled up a tiresome ascent of 1000 feet to Aardee, a small hamlet on the slope of the mountain, thence to Koorgoo, and at length turned the shoulder of the range at an elevation of 2500 feet above the Munglaad river. From near the summit I arranged the Theodolite and amused myself in taking the angles of depression of some of the places which we had passed. The sango was depressed 33°, the hamlet of Aardee 37°, and Mujjowlee 12°. After surmounting this fatiguing ascent we went through cornfields and woods for two miles, and reached Sooraan at 8 A. M.

Sooraan is the summer residence of the Rajah of Bussheer. It is pleasantly situated on a wooded ridge from the Himalaya, which sweeps dow nto the Sutluj three miles distant. On the right bank of this river the mountains rise abruptly to a great altitude, and are covered with snow. The Shatool Pass is only twelve miles from here. It is said to bear S. E. The glen of the Sutluj trends eastward, the river flowing westward, and forcing its way through the snowy mountains.

The buildings at Sooraan may be called handsome, for in this country much is not to be expected. The edifice most deserving of notice is a temple close to the Rajah's residence which consists of several houses. They are all in the Chinese style, with pent-roofs, balconies, and some beautifully-carved wood, which have, if nothing more, at least novelty to give them effect. The temple is dedicated to Kalee. It is surmounted with gilt ornaments. We were informed that human sacrifices were offered here in former times to this goddess, but have been discontinued since the expulsion of the Goorkas.

A few miles beyond Sooraan to the eastward is the boundary between Dussow and Koonawr, which latter district reaches to Chinese Tartary, and is subject to Bussheer. It is said that there are no officiating Brahmins in the temples beyond our present quarters, so that we have reached the utmost limit of their religion in this direction.

26th May, *Sooraan.*—Having heard that there were hot springs, called the Augoon Koond, near the bed of the Sutluj, we walked down this morning to see them. They bear from Sooraan 318°, with an angle of 19° of depression. The distance by the road is three miles, and nearly 4000 feet below the place where we have pitched our bechobas. They issue from the side of a dell through which an impetuous stream rolls, about half a mile from the Sutluj. This torrent forms a fine cascade, bounding over a narrow rent in a mass of gneiss, and falling about 40 feet. The springs are five in number, and are all within the length of fifteen paces. The principal one gushes from beneath a projecting rock close to the waterfall, and runs into a small artificial well of mica-slate, which has been made for pilgrims to bathe in. The water is clear, hot, smoking, and has a saline taste, but no smell. The pebbles it passes over are of mica-slate, which it coats with a ferruginous matter. The spot from whence it issues is thickly incrusted with a white salt. The hot vapour issuing from the springs, has considerably decomposed the rock above, depositing in it particles of a yellow substance, not unlike sulphur, although there is no sulphureous smell emitted about the place. I bathed in the well, but could scarcely bear the heat of the water. The quantity which flows during the day from these sources must be very great, as a brass vessel whose contents were equal to 2 lbs. was filled from the principal rill in seven seconds.

By the time we reached our little tents, which were pitched near a walnut-tree, we were too tired to make any other excursion, and therefore contented ourselves with admiring the scenery and sketching. I also took a few observations with the theodolite. The most eastern snowy peak across the Sutluj bore N. 25° 51′ E., with an angle of 8° 54′ of elevation, and an estimated distance of 15 miles. Another snowy peak bore N.W. by W., distant perhaps 20 miles. Upon this side of the river some patches of snow lay upon the mountains, bearing S. E. by E., distant three miles.

28th May, *Gowra,* 11 m. 4 f.—We quitted Sooraan at 4 h. 45 m. A. M. and reached Gowra at 8 h. 30 m. A. M. As the Rajah was at Mujjowlee we were permitted to occupy the house which he has here. Some cherries were brought to us, but they were small and bitter.

We left Sooraan with regret, for it is a pleasant spot, and is, besides, the most eastern point of the Sutluj, as well as the highest northern latitude that I shall perhaps ever reach in India. This is an unpleasant reflection to us all, for we are charmed with the grandeur and the refreshing coolness of this country. During our walk to Gowra we saw the snowy heights of the Himalaya above, and beyond Wangtoo on the Sutluj. They are indeed magnificence personified, and tower in such massive pinnacles, that they seem as if they would overbalance the finely poised earth. The Snowy Range on the left bank of this river we have only seen occasionally since leaving Wartoo.

In the part of the mountains we are now in, no

wheel-carriages can be used, and goonts are seldom seen; the Rajah, indeed, had a few at Sooraan, but it was a matter of infinite surprise to us, considering the abruptness of the foot-path, and the frailty of the sangos, how they were ever brought there.

The villages in Bussheer are very neat; they are also cleanly, which is singular, for mountaineers are proverbially a careless race. We have only seen swine about them twice.

29th May, *Rampoor*, 8 m. 4 f.—Whilst we were at Gowra, yesterday evening, the clouds, that had lately covered the mountains, dispersed slowly, and we saw through their enormous vistas, the snowy Himalaya beyond the Sutluj vastly distinct, until at length the whole range was revealed upon the deep sky, fixed in monumental stillness. Beneath the dazzlingly white broad slope of snows, a black mural precipice hung like a huge dark pall down to the Sutluj, while the nearer mountains crested with pines, and broken into ridges and chasms, were steeped in inestimably rich blue dyes. The sight was almost unreal.

30th May, *Koteghur*, 20 m. 4 f,—We rode to the foot of the Gaut within five miles of Koteghur. The Sutluj was greatly swollen by the rapid melting of the snows, and rolled down the glen with an eye-straining velocity. Pine-trees which had fallen into it, were hurled along with a swiftness that was surprising. We frequently watched one, and starting fairly, cantered as fast as our goonts would go, to keep up with it; but in vain, it always outstripped us. The races were ludicrous.

Throwing off our upper clothes, and leaving the goonts, we began the toilsome ascent. The sun blazed upon the side of the mountain, the air was breathless, and the heat was intolerable; we, however, gained at length the summit, and passing the old fort of Joudpoor, descended through corn-fields and woods to a cool, cool stream, which runs below Koteghur, and plunging our heads into it, completely refreshed ourselves. From hence an ascent of a few hundred feet brought us, after traversing another pine-forest, to a more temperate region and to those we had left.

After we had seen our friends and attendants, we were glad to rest a little; and, as our excursion to the Boorendo was the next principal object, we sat down and discussed the matter at some length. Sooraan, and the places we had already visited, furnished also a portion of our conversation. It was now evening, and the majestic view before us charmed us into silence. The nearer hills appeared like swelling shadows in an ocean of ethereal purple. As range upon range rose higher and higher, the tints grew more delicate and natural; and those upon which the sun still shone were vivid and instinct with brightness. Above them rose the massive yet airy deserts and peaks of eternal snow. There is nothing so soothing to the mind as the loveliness of creation combined with vastness and tranquillity. It was before us. As the sun declined, in one brief instant the whiteness of the Snowy Range vanished, and it appeared glowing in the majesty of glory, like an immeasurable and stupendous wilderness of rocks of gold!

Then as the sun sunk deeper, hue upon hue

of the lesser ranges verged into uniformity; still the lofty pinnacles of the Himalaya shone in rich splendour. They too at length grew shadowy, and indistinct, and were at last gradually obliterated by the all-presiding darkness of night.

CHAPTER V.

KOTEGHUR TO THE BOORENDO PASS.

4th June, *Koteghur.*—We have been in the midst of bustle and confusion since our return from Sooraan, on account of our preparations for the journey to the Boorendo Pass. Much foresight was required in order to provide, not only for our own wants, but for those also of our host of followers; for we were to travel through wildness and desolation, and over dangerous and difficult paths. Besides the luxuries we had determined upon taking with us, grain in abundance was to be procured and packed for our attendants. Even firewood was to be carried when we should ascend beyond the limits of vegetation; and as no four-footed animals, with the exception of sheep, are ever employed, from the narrowness of the routes, which are little better than sheep-walks, to cross the hither Himalayan Passes, and as we had determined not to use them for the burdens, there arose perpetual discussions among the porters respecting their loads, for they well knew the labour they were about to undergo. However, by carefully examining the physical force of each individual, and speaking kindly, we found them very reasonable; and observed no wish on their part to load their better-natured fellows for their own especial benefit. Experience had taught them that mutual assistance was the foundation of all success. When we had settled their apportionments, our next difficulty was to fix upon those of our domestics who were to remain at Koteghur with the women and children, and also to take charge of the goonts and baggage. All appeared anxious to accompany their masters in what seemed a service of danger, and we had much ado to quiet the importunity of the rejected. These preliminaries being adjusted, and the Boorendo Pass reported practicable, we were at length ready. The party consisted of Capt. A. Gerard, and P.

Gerard, Major Close, Lieut. Osborne, and myself. The first two gentlemen were experienced and veteran Himalayan travellers; confiding therefore in their knowledge, we anticipated no difficulty but the toil.

5th June, *Sheyl*, 10m. 4f., elevation 8000 feet. —The sky was clear, and the air pure and bracing, as we started from Koteghur this morning up the road to Wartoo, and continued our ascent till we passed Jurrool. We there struck off upon a foot-path to the left, crossed a shoulder of Wartoo, increasing our elevation 1700 feet, and then descended 700 feet into a deep glen, throngh which ran a delicious stream of water. This spot was peculiarly refreshing, being shaded by fine handsome trees from the intense heat of the sun. The fort of Wartoo was only a short distance on our right, though very high above us. From this stream we had a sharp rise of 1000 feet, and from thence a descent to Noon, which is a small village embosomed in fields. It is about six or seven miles from Koteghur. Continuing our descent, we came to another stream, 1800 feet lower, from whence we toiled over fragments of mica-slate to the ruinous fort of Bajee, which is upon a spur of Wartoo. Its elevation is 9105 feet. This was a most fatiguing ascent of 2300 feet. Bajee is commanded on all sides, and as a military post, it is of little importance. The ridge on which it is built, runs to the N. E., and joins the Snowy Mountains. Nawaghur is another old fort, on a peak of the same ridge, about three or four miles to the N. E. From Bajee we saw a branch of Wartoo trend southwards, separating the Girree and Cheegaon rivers, and there terminating. Descending 1100 feet from Bajee, we came to Sheyl, 1 m. 4 f. by the road, dreadfully fatigued, and some of us making very sore complaints of very sore feet.

There is a good deal of tillage, and several neat hamlets about Sheyl, which is in a pleasant situation, though the mountains in its vicinity hide the Himalaya. They are, nevertheless, very picturesque, having beautiful pine-forests upon their sides and along their crests, while greensward, dotted with elegant trees and luxuriant bushes, sweeps from wood to wood, broken here and there by the gray rifted rock. The deep glen of the Cheegaon, with one of its flanks richly cultivated, adds also to the beauty of the scene, which is mellowed by the radiant azure of the sky.

We saw the Choor Pahar from Bajee, bearing almost due south. It had scarcely a vestige of snow upon it.

Our track lay, the whole of the march, through a magnificent forest, chiefly of cedars and pines, which afforded a most grateful shade. A little below Noon we reached a rudely-made Goont-road, which leads from Koteghur to Teekur. We could not perceive a spot of snow upon Wartoo. During the march we saw the peaks of the hither Himalaya towering up from both banks of the Sutluj, glittering like immense freshly-riven masses of alabaster. Nothing less than seeing them in their native, pure atmosphere, can give a conception of their exceeding brightness. We also recognised in the range the Shatool Pass, and the mountains above Sooraan. In the woods we found the wild red rose. The prevailing rock was mica-slate.

Thermometer at sunrise 59°, Fahr. at Koteghur.
„ highest 74°, „ at Sheyl.
„ lowest 60°, „ „

6th June, *Kusshain,* 9 m. 4 f., elevation 6800 feet.—Immediately upon leaving Sheyl we descended 800 feet, crossed the Cheegaon river, and began to ascend the ridge which connects the Choor Pahar with Wartoo. Our way was through fine masses of cedar, pine, and oak, and over a profusion of flowers and strawberries springing from the sward, and refreshing rills, all which made us forget an ascent of 2700 feet to the summit of the Sooraar gaut. The elevation of this pass is 9900 feet. It is of gneiss. From this high point a majestic prospect appeared. The Himalaya, always sublime, and the lower hills, formed a tangled heap that half filled the sky. In the profound valley below we perceived the stone fort of Teekur, upon a ridge which protruded direct from the one on which we stood. The sides of this broad ravine were richly covered with corn, interspersed with numerous hamlets, and from the base as it were of this skiey depth, though afar, rose the three peaks of Jumnootree in angelic stateliness to the cope of heaven! On their right, the pinnacles, as we conjectured, in the vicinity of Gungootree, towered nobly, though faded by distance. Far on the left of the Jumnootree peaks, the pyramidal Raaldung peered over the crest of the Snowy Range. In front, and to the left, we looked down into the glen of the Pubbur, running up to the Boorendo Pass, filled with heaving mists, and grasped by two hoary arms of the Himalaya. We then remarked the wide and steep snowy planes, and craggy summits of the Shatool Pass, with the Hunsbusshum peak close to them, which seemed to tremble in its attempt to reach the skies. As this was the nearest part of the Snowy Chain to us, it appeared almost to rival the exalted peaks of Jumnootree. The scene was closed by the Himalaya beyond the Sutluj. We also saw from here Kurroll near Subahtoo, Mahhasoo, Shaalee, the Choor Pahar, Wartoo, Seelajaan above Koteghur, and the mountains near Sooraan. It is no matter of surprise that our Fathers of old worshipped GOD on the mountain-tops!

We remained on this elevated point, which is four miles from Sheyl, for an hour, and then continuing our journey along the ridge, upon a turf of the most delicate green embroidered with lovely blossoms for a mile, turned short to the left, and descended, gradually, to the ruined fort of Teekur. On the right we looked down into the fertile Purgunnah of Kotegooroo. Another mile, from the fort of Teekur, brought us to Kusshain. We had in this distance decreased our elevation 3100 feet.

Whilst our bechobas were being pitched, we sat down under a mulberry-tree, and were soon surrounded by the Naawur men, who brought us milk, and behaved with the greatest kindness. Naawur is a district of the Bussheer Rauj. The disposition of its inhabitants is warlike, and consequently, trouble is often met with in collecting the State tribute. The men are by no means handsome. They have sallow complexions, affect beards, are rather tall, and seem active. Many of the young women are very pretty. The costume of both sexes is the same as that worn by the people of Koteghur, Rampoor, and Sooraan.

They are here getting in their harvest. The corn is cut, as in other parts of the hills we have visited, with the sickle. It is then brought home and laid upon the roofs to dry, and the grain is trodden out by bullocks, which are muzzled with small wicker baskets during the operation.

At Sheyl a large pannier of snow was brought as a present from Naawaghur, and at this place a similar gift was made.

Kusshain is a large and neat village; indeed, it is the principal one in Naawur. The view from it is confined by the surrounding mountains, which, as they are barely wooded, are not very picturesque. Near the village are iron-mines, which we visited in the evening, and procured specimens of the mineral, which is micaceous iron-ore. The mines are worked by running a horizontal shaft, only 3½ feet in diameter, into the side of the mountain, the formation of which is mica-slate. The ore is brought out in skins, reduced to a fine powder, washed in a little stream, and smelted. When reduced into small pigs, it is again put into the fire, and hammered until it becomes malleable. All these processes are performed upon the spot. The furnaces are nothing more than large clay crucibles, about three feet high, not unlike two inverted cones with the diameter in the centre, of about eighteen inches. There are two holes at the bottom, for the insertion of the nozzles of two bellows. The crucible, being placed over an ash-hole, is filled with the pounded ore, fire applied, and the bellows worked. When this is sufficiently fused, an iron rod is struck through the bottom of the crucible, upon the withdrawal of which, the impurities run into the ash-pit, leaving the iron in the crucible. This was the process described to us. It is said that these mines are scarcely worth working.

In the evening, we tried the experiment of finding the elevation by the temperature at which water boils. Upon putting the thermometer into boiling water the mercury rose to 201°.5, which is two degrees too much, there being a known error to that amount in the instrument used. Therefore, deducting 199°.5, which was the true point at which water boiled here, from 212°, which is the boiling-point at the sea-level, there was left 12°.5 for the difference. This, being multiplied by 550 feet (550 feet = 1° Fahrenheit), gave 6875 feet as the elevation of Kusshain, which was very nearly the same as the barometrical measurement. In fact, if the proper corrections had been applied, it would have approached nearer to the true measurement. The scale of our thermometer was Fahrenheit's.

Thermometer, highest 83°, lowest 57°.5, Fahr.

7th June, *Rooroo,* 10 m. 4 f., elevation 5171 feet.—We began our walk by descending through corn-fields until we arrived at the precipitous banks of a rapid stream 600 feet below Kusshain, which we crossed upon a broad plank thirty feet in length and high over it. At this point, which is six furlongs from Kusshain, we passed the vil lage of Narrain, which is on a high wooded crag, overhanging the confluence of two torrents. It is a wild view. The next villages we came to were

Sheekul, 1 m. 1 f. Teekurree 6 f. further, Koro 3 f.; and 3 f. more brought us to a stream at the foot of the Punneeout gaut. The elevation of this stream is 6500 feet. We here commenced our usual task of climbing. To the summit of the Pass is 1511 feet, and 1 mile by the road, which is very slippery, and over a bare mountain-ridge, composed of mica-slate, that divides Naawur from Mundulghur. When we gained the crest we were disappointed in the view, for the elevation is 8011 feet. The valley of the Pubbur lay before us, running from E. N. E. to W. S. W., formed by two enormous twisted roots of the Himalaya. That on the left bank, which was to our right as we looked up the stream, is called the Changsheel Range. Its elevation, as it descends, mantled with snow, from the Great Chain, varies from 15,000 ft. to 9000 ft. Over it are several passes, which cross to the valley of the Gosangro, a torrent rising near the Rupin Pass, which leads over the Himalaya, to Sungla in the valley of the Buspa. The Gosangro at length falls into the Tonse. On the right bank is the Moraal or Imraal Range.

These two send off jagged ridges, which run down in broken masses to the bed of the Pubbur, which we could follow with our eyes almost to its junction with the Tonse. Above the highest part of the Pubbur valley, to the left, peered the immense steep snowy steps of the Shatool. To the S. W. the view was confined by the lofty Sirgool Ridge with its shivered summits crested with trees, and flanks wood-clad and dark, dappled with a few patches of snow. This ridge traverses the Joobul State, and joins the one we crossed yesterday by the Sooraar Gaut.

From the Punneeout Pass we descended 2840 ft., sometimes gradually, sometimes abruptly, to Rooroo, passing through a good deal of cultivation, and remarking several villages to the left in the midst of corn-fields. Raal 4 f. from the road, and 3 m. 4 f. from Rooroo, was the largest of them; we also saw the Fort of Raaen, where we have a small garrison, on the left bank of the Pubbur, about seven or eight miles lower down the river.

Rooroo is a considerable village in the Chooaara district. It is on the western shore, and about

200 ft. above the stream, which sends down a large body of water into the Tonse. The river-bed is about 200 paces wide, though the current itself is not more than thirty paces. It is very rapid, and above the town is divided into several little channels. The temperature of the water was 52°.5 Fahrenheit. Our followers procured an abundance of grain, which the inhabitants, having received intelligence of our visit, had provided.

The valley of the Pubbur at Rooroo is from a mile to a mile and a quarter in width. Looking towards the Himalaya, the mountains sweep down to the river with their terraced bases girdled with yellow crops, in which are many hamlets, though we perceive others nestled among the heights above. Dark pines patch the slopes, or fringe the gray shattered crags of the ridges: the ravines are filled with bushy woods, or covered with exquisitely green sward, and through the midst the Pubbur rolls among disjointed blocks, or rapidly rushes over pebbles, with an intemperate sound that harmonizes fully with the grandeur of the scene. Above this and far, rise mountain-ranges of a deep purple, strangely interwoven with each other, whose peaks are blanched with snow. There is richness in the corn, wildness in the rocks, sublimity in the extent, magnificence in all.

A little below Rooroo the stream of the Pubbur glides with amazing but imperceptible velocity. The servant who had charge of the geese we had brought with us for that useful purpose which that cunning philosopher, Sancho Panza, defines as "belly timber," seduced by the apparent tranquillity of the waters, which passed like a mass of purest crystal, and the benevolence of his heart for the long-cooped prisoners, determined, in consideration of the briefness of their vitality, to indulge them with a bathe. He opened the pannier smiling, and heard with a laugh their grateful hisses as they stretched their long necks, and waddled with swift gravity into the river. But, alas! no sooner were they in, than the treacherous eddies whirled them round, and swept them away with curious rapidity. The man was alarmed. His laugh was petrified on his face.

The astonished geese attempted to steer across the stream, but they were whirled along by the ruthless spirits of the Pubbur. The keeper urged his two wearied legs to their utmost speed, to recapture the cackling host, but long and arduous was his chase before he could, either by short-breathed entreaties, or failing grasps, rescue them from their unnatural death, for they had lost all self-possession and were going at a death's express towards the Tonse, in which they would inevitably have been consigned to a watery grave, and doubtless have had their bones sepulchred by the little fishes in the Jumna. He, however, re-seized them. His delight was inexpressible, nay, perhaps he wept for joy, and in the womanish dimness of his eyes, mistook them for fellow-creatures.

We fished in the Pubbur and also in the Sheekree, a stream which comes from the N. W. and joins close to the village here. We found near here the Baubool, a shrub common on the plains.

Thermometer, highest 92° Fahrenheit.

" lowest 58° at daybreak 8th June.

8th June, *Cheergaon*, 11 m. 2 f., elevation 5985 feet.—There are two roads from Rooroo to Cheergaon, the better along the left bank of the Pubbur, crossing the river by a sango opposite Rooroo, and returning to the right bank at Mandlee by a similar bridge, where it joins the other road.

It was doubtful if the sango were now set at Mandlee, for at this season of the year they are often taken down, from the fear of sudden floods sweeping them away; we therefore determined to proceed by the route upon the right bank, which was represented to us as being much more difficult.

We left Rooroo at 4 h. 20 m. A. M., and in an hour passed Seema, a hamlet of two or three houses, which nevertheless appears to have been a larger place formerly. There was a delicious well there. At 5 h. 50 m. we were in front of Buttoolee, a small fort and village on the other side of the river to us, and about a mile distant. It is upon a low hill, with high mountains behind it covered with woods. Whilst near it a broad blazing sunbeam swept over the place, and formed for a short time a splendid view. At 6 h. 5 m. we crossed the Berreear upon some spars that fenced a fish-weir. This torrent comes from the N. W. and with such force that it is not fordable. At 6 h. 40 m, we were at Mandlee, opposite the large village of Massoolee. We went to look at the sango over the Pubbur, and crossed it. It is thirty feet long, three feet broad, and twelve or fifteen feet above the current, which is very impetuous, so much so in fact, that it is advisable not to look at it, but fix the eye upon some object on the opposite side. Massoolee is prettily situated. It seems to be in a flourishing condition. Re-crossing to Mandlee we continued our walk, and reached the small hamlet of Soonda at 7 h. 8 m., and Bowerkotee at 7 h. 23 m. Ten minutes from thence brought us to the Undrittee river, which we crossed on two planks 25 feet in length, and high above the stream. This sango is a dangerous one, as the spars are slight, and sway up and down from the weight of the body, as well as from the roaring rush of the torrent. The Undrittee rises near the Shatool, or Roll

Pass, 24 m. distant, rivals the Pubbur in size, and joins it near Bowerkotee. The scene up the glen through which it tumbles, though not extensive, is very picturesque. A gigantic ridge from the Himala, covered with snow, and 10 m. distant, is the back-ground; the sides of the dell are varied with trees and tillage, and deep in the midst, the Undrittee, thickly besprent with foam, hurries along furiously. At 7 h. 40 m. we reached Cheergaon, and pitched our bechobas amongst apricot-trees close to the village, which is a poor place in the Chooara district.

We find the valley of the Pubbur decrease very perceptibly in width as we advance. Our road, which was as usual a mere foot-path, followed the river closely the whole way, nor had we ascents or descents that were at all considerable to encounter; but when opposite to Buttoolee, the crags descended abruptly into the current. We stopped in surprise; the guide, however, picked his way along their precipitous sides, and we followed with great caution. A little further, the rock overhung the river, which tore its way through the glen with a thundering noise, and bedazzled with spray; here the path was lost. Looking anxiously at the bare block, we perceived little notches, large enough for our toes to rest upon. Pulling off our shoes and jackets, we embraced the smooth mass as widely as we could, stretched out our legs to secure the precarious footing, and thus passed this dangerous spot with the utmost ease. One of the camp-followers, we learnt afterwards, was not so fortunate. He fell into the fearful chasm, and was drowned. Peace be with him! for I have travelled sufficiently to feel, that of what creed soever we may be the followers, we are not the less brethren. When safely over, the guide pointed out another path, which led along the cliffs, 800 feet above us. It was by this that most of our party and the baggage came.

The glen of the Pubbur, at Cheergaon, is about half a mile broad, bounded at its extremity by ridges from the Himala, covered with snow. They seem to be eight or ten miles from hence.

My feet were very much blistered already, and

the pain they gave me in walking, made me very feverish to-day; but as the Boorendo Pass, the great object of our curiosity, was only four marches from here, I was induced to remain quiet in the tent, as I had no inclination to be left behind. This circumstance prevented my making any inquiries as to Cheergaon.

Thermometer, highest 91° lowest 64° Fahrenheit,

9th June, *Sustwar* or *Pekka,* 11 m. elevation 8759 feet.—I set off alone, at 4 A. M., and reached Sustwar, in the Pekka Purgunnah, at 11 A. M. My guides, active lads of eighteen, gave me the choice of two roads, the upper and the lower. I preferred the former, being tempted by the hopes of a cooler climate, for the valley of the Pubbur was insufferably hot. It led through the purgunnahs of Kaubool, Konniaro, and Pekka. I discovered afterwards that it was three miles longer than the other.

I was unwell, and could not walk with lightness, which was the reason I was so long on the route. We began by ascending to the village of

Dinwaaree, which we reached at 5 h. 55 m. It is about 2000 feet above Cheergaon. The side of the mountain was very rugged, and in many places the path along the crags so hazardous, the danger being made much greater, by my illness, that I was forced occasionally to allow myself to be guided by the young men. The next village I arrived at was Kaubool, the elevation of which is 8400 feet. This was at 6 h. 40 m. I had ascended 2415 feet. From Kaubool I passed through five more villages, and arrived at the Bechobas quite tired. The country, almost the whole way, was well tilled, and the villages large, clean, and delightfully situated amongst shady trees. The sycamore, chestnut, and apricot, the last loaded with green fruit, grew in great luxuriance. Numerous streams likewise rushed down the sides of the mountain, and either turned mills, or were conducted to irrigate the fields. Most of the places I passed through, on my route, were at elevations of between 8000 and 9000 feet. The land does not appear to be cultivated higher. Above this are pine-woods of great size, beyond them sward, and finally, rock capped with snow. The villagers were frank and kind to me. Many of the women were very handsome. Their complexions are fair and blushing. All the hamlets in the Bussheer Rauj are guarded by a breed of very fierce dogs, peculiar to the mountains. They are large and strong, with wool beneath the hair. They have bushy tails, and their colour is usually black, red, or white.

At a spot called Chandee Daar, which is about a mile from Sustwar, the path skirted the edge of the highest cliffs I ever saw. The Pubbur foamed in the narrowed glen 4000 feet below the mural precipice, upon the crest of which we walked. At this point, as once before to-day, my head became slightly affected by dizziness, and I was consequently obliged to take hold of the guides' hands till I had passed it. It is extraordinary, nay, almost inconceivable, that a trifling indisposition should so totally derange the nervous system, that one trembles to look at those fearful places, which, when in health, would be the cause of high admiration.

Sustwar is a small hamlet on the mountains forming the left side of the glen of the Pubbur, looking up towards the Himala. There are five villages in the vicinity. On the Changsheel range which forms the right side of the glen the snow lies thickly, though in the surrounding ravines it is fast melting, forming rills which vault from rock to rock till they plunge into the river below. The view is very confined, for not a single peak of the Snowy Range is visible from here, nor indeed from Cheergaon or Rooroo. One of the pinnacles of the spiry Changsheel Ridge near us rises to an elevation of 13,500 ft. Below on the opposite side we see some patches of snow.

If the natives are asked the name of this place, they answer Pekka, which is the name of the Purgunnah. We saw two very beautiful girls here. The natives of these more elevated districts wear a black conical cap, which has a tassel on the top, and is puckered at the bottom. We feasted upon strawberries on the road, and singularly enough, I had not been long at Sustwar before my indisposition vanished, and I felt strong and active again.

Thermometer, highest 79°.

" do 92° in the sun's rays.

" lowest 60°.5 cloudy morning.

10th June, *Jangleeg*, 6 m. 2 f. elevat. 9300 ft. —We commenced our journey this morning at 4 h. 15 m. by a gradual ascent through fields of corn, and at 4 h. 50 m. we saw, from the ridge we were crossing, the Himalaya, apparently ten miles distant, closing the dell of the Pubbur. On the right the Changsheel Range rose precipitously from the bed of the river. Its sides were nevertheless hung with pine-woods, and it was truly astonishing to see them grasping the fissured rocks with their roots, and from the scantiest moisture flourishing luxuriantly. Many were fallen into the stream, and others across it, forming natural sangos. Above the limit of forest were large wastes of snow. On the left, and it was along this side that we were journeying, the mountains sloped sharply to the river, but were, nevertheless, well cultivated, and adorned with noble deodars, oaks, sycamores, and other trees. We could also see from this spot the confine of the arborescent vegetation, beyond which was a rich and vivid green sward overtopped with immense snow-beds, broken and mottled, dissolving evidently very fast. But how magnificent did the Snowy Range appear now that we were close to it!

One of the spotless peaks of the Yoosoo Pass, that has an elevation of 17,000 feet, towered majestically, and there were besides in that direction vast slopes of snow inclining to the S. E. Immediately before us was the village of Jangleeg, on the wooded promontory which overhangs the junction of the Seepun and the Pubbur. At 5 h. 30 m. we reached Deodee, or rather a hamlet in the Purgunnah of that name. It is a wild spot, surrounded by handsome deodars, chestnuts, and oaks. From hence we descended gradually to a torrent that joins the Pubbur, a few yards distant on the right. We crossed it by a spar, and stopped a short time to indulge our admiration of the scene. At 6 h. 50 m. we came to the confluence of the

Seepun and the Pubbur; here the enormous gneiss rocks rise sheer several hundred feet into mural precipices, over which many cascades formed from the melting of the snows tumble into the gulf below, which has been riven asunder by the uncontrollable cataracts. The ravines through which they dash are deep; that of the Pubbur skirted by quivering crags splintered into sharp pinnacles, and both, darkened into abysses of gloom, filled with whirlwinds of the whitest mists, and re-echoing the hollow thunders of the eternally vexed torrents, which seem like the revelling laughters of desolation. This is Himalayan grandeur, inspiring awe breathless with delight and wonder!

The elevation of the confluence is 8300 feet. There is a sango over the Seepun, at this place, of two narrow planks, thirty-four feet in length, and about twelve or fifteen feet above the impatient current. Here some of our followers seemed to want resolution to cross the perilous bridge. One crawled over on his hands and knees, another sat astride, and urged himself over by his hands, while others were led by the vice-like grasp of their comrades. A Pariah dog that had followed us from the Plains, and was a favourite with the camp-people, who had given him, on account of his enterprising disposition, the cognomen of Subahtoo, was however so frightened, that he would not hazard himself on so insecure a footing, and howled piteously at being left behind; one of the mountaineers re-crossed and carried him over in his arms.

The Seepun comes from the Yoosoo Pass, the Pubbur from the Boorendo, and though they are neither more than twelve miles distant, yet, from the large volume of water in each stream, one would suppose they had already traversed a hundred miles before they met. The declivity of the Pubbur between here and Cheergaon is 254 feet in a mile. We halted for a half-hour to enjoy the sublimity of this extraordinary spot, and then climbed a steep and rocky ascent of 1000 feet to Jangleeg. Our bechobas were pitched under some fine shady chestnuts, upon rather a level piece of ground; it was one of the finest encampments we had made since quitting Koteghur. The prospect from it is very confined. The ridge of the mountain we are upon is partially cultivated, but its produce, the paapur, is still green, and there are doubts as to its ripening this year. Above the fields are large woods of stately cedars, oaks, and pines. It is now that we have reached the last habitable part of this side of the hither Himala. There are, in the Purgunnah we are now in, six villages, all near to each other. They are miserable-looking dwellings, but we have been particularly pleased with the frank, cheerful, hospitable, and spirited conduct of the inhabitants. The latter, indeed, was shown, upon one of our attendants entering a house and stealing some grain; he was soon discovered, and seized by two old men, who dragged him before us.

We have just learnt a new fashion of smoking, which is as follows:—A piece of stick was thrust into the ground at a little depth, and turned upwards again to the surface, so as to make a narrow channel three or four inches from its insertion. A hollow reed was then placed upright into one of the orifices, while the other was filled with tobacco and lighted, and we smoked as comfortably as with a pipe. What strange devices necessity invents! The world turned into a dhudeen!*

It rained heavily in the evening, and many and conflicting were the opinions regarding the weather, a most important consideration, as, for the three next days, we were to be without the limits of human habitations. However, being confined to our little tent, and having nothing better to do, we let the rain rattle, and determined to pass away the time by feasting and laughing. When we had dined we sent for two or three of the wild old men of Jangleeg for the purpose of inquiring what they, more conversant with the fickleness of the seasons here, thought of the likelihood of sunshine and of the state of the Boorendo. They came; their tanned-looking persons clothed in dark brown sooklaat, with the black conical

* "In Wales an old seasoned clay-pipe is more highly valued than a new one; and with smokers of shag, more especially those of the Sister Isle, a *dhudeen*—a short pipe, so called in Irish from its black colour."—*A Paper:—of Tobacco.* London: Chapman & Hall, 1839.

cap peculiar to the district, and armed with bows and arrows of bamboo, the only warlike weapon they use. Upon their entrance they saluted us with much courtesy, and sat down with the profound gravity of simplicity. We then asked them touching the weather. They replied that our only chance was to offer sacrifices to the Deotas, or Mountain Spirits, as a means of favourable propitiation; to which we at once assented, and announced that we would perform the rites after our custom. They appeared somewhat alarmed at this readiness, fearing that the Deotas we worshipped might quarrel with theirs, and thus expose them to the perpetual anger of both, which would ensure a triple quantity of rocks rolling about their ears, as well as new-invented blights for their paapur crops, the loosening of dangerous sangos, piercing winds, redoubled frosts, and horrible noises in the passes they were so often obliged to cross, but we without delay commenced our incantations by closing the tent. The old men arose. Two plates filled with a mixture of brandy and salt, with a solitary candle, were put upon the table. We at the same time began mumbling the uncouthest sounding words that we could invent, and then, slowly increasing the chant, fired the spirit, suddenly dashed down the candle, and in violent paroxysms dipped our fingers into the fires, and then put them flaring into our mouths. The countenances of all were blanched. Nothing was heard but the pattering of the rain, and the hurtling of the flames as we swung our blazing hands to and fro, till at length we flung the flaming plates to the top of the tent, when all was instantaneously dark, and the sages of Jangleeg rushed out terrified, amidst the peals of our inspired laughter, almost upsetting the bechoba in their bewildered anxiety.

Bearings, &c. from Jangleeg.

	Bearing.	Ang. Elev.	Est. Dis.	Height. Feet.
Farthest Peak up the glen	65°	11° 21′	4 m. 0 f.	4157
Kusshain Peak	102°	24° 15′	2 m. 0 f.	4338
Deota Peak............	135°	29° 0	6 f.	1920

The above are the spiry shattered peaks of the Changsheel ridge, which separates the glen of the Pubbur from that of the Roopin. The height of the Kusshain peak, we know already to be 13,800 feet. I merely put down these heights, not so much for accuracy, as for the purpose of illustrating the wild scenery at Jangleeg.

Temperature of the Pubbur 40°, Fahrenheit.

Thermometer, highest 67°, lowest 49°, Fahrenheit.

11th June, Camp at the *Leetee Torrent,* 7 m. 4 f., elevation 11,692 feet.—Our incantations had produced the desired effect, for the air this morning was of a celestial purity. We left Jangleeg at 8 A. M., and reached the Leetee at 11 h. 20 m. A. M. The first part of our journey was a steep ascent over gneiss rocks. At 8 h. 30 m. we came to a shepherd's hut, the last habitation, and that merely a temporary one. From this spot we perceived, on the right side of the Pubbur dell, snow-patches, 200 or 300 feet below us. At 9 h. 24 m. we passed over large shattered blocks of gneiss, which had been precipitated by some gigantic convulsion from the cliffs on the left. In fact, it seemed as though we were in the midst of a noiseless torrent of rocks. At 9 h. 40 m. we quitted the wood of pine and birch, through which we had been tracking our way, and beheld the snowy cradle of the Pubbur over-canopied by a craggy ridge of the Himalaya. To the right, the fretted pinnacles of the Changsheel range towered aloft into the azure dome of heaven, the ravines on their torn sides filled with snow and the ruins of avalanches, while beneath, at their feet, the Pubbur bounded along, robed in a mantle of foam. To the left, the broad flank of the mountains sloped to the river, covered with brilliantly green sward, and mosaicked with lovely, and many of them, to us, unknown flowers. Over this our path ran, but, from the swell of the mountain above us, our view on that side was very confined. At 10 h. 10 m. we crossed the first patches of snow, and a torrent, which rushes from a wooded glen, chiefly of cedars and birches, on the left, joining the Pubbur a few yards from us on the right. At 10 h. 30 m. we passed through a similar glen, only the stream from it was greatly hidden by a snow-bed. It also falls into the Pubbur. At 11 h. 20 m. we were upon the right bank of the Leetee torrent, and shortly after had our bechobas pitched at its junction with the Pubbur.

Since leaving the last glen we remarked the birches dwindling in size near the brink of the Pubbur, and now not one is seen on the left side of the dell, though upon the Changsheel ridge, which forms the right side, they run up in the ravines 800 feet above us, or to an elevation of about 12,500 feet. We have thus reached the line of limited forest on the southern flank of the Himala. Before us is a region of rock and snow.

The path between Jangleeg and this place offers no difficulty to harass the passer. The ascent, too, is generally gradual. But upon the opposite side, beneath the Changsheel peaks, if it were even possible to make a track, there would be constant danger, for, from the perpetual changes of frost and thaw, the rocks are fissured, loosened, and then, by their weight, they break with a thunder-crash, and hurl downwards, followed and following heaps of ruin into the Pubbur.

The prospect around is sublime. On our left the Leetee rolls over a broken ridge of fine-grained gneiss, in a noble cascade, and is immediately buried beneath a bed of snow. Beside it, the gray peaks of the Himalaya rise precipitously, while, at their bases, are strewn massive splinters and crushed fragments. Before us, the dell of the Pubbur rests upon the parent Snowy Range, where all but some black mural precipices of rock, is an eternity of refulgent whiteness. It is over one of these gloomy walls that the Pubbur plunges into a snow-bed beneath, rivalling the Leetee in form and magnificence. Above, one of the Passes is marked by a stupendous peak. But the sublimest objects of this sublimest scene of savage grandeur, are on our right. These are the mighty peaks that bound the Umrain Pass, springing in naked majesty from the Changsheel or Kusshain ridge, which is a torn wilderness of sterility. The heavens are of the deepest dye, the air as pure as at the Creation, and as still; and so vividly does every thing appear, that it seems of a frailty which the merest motion of the hand would shatter to pieces!

I walked to the Leetee waterfall with my

friend Osborne. It is full a mile and a half from our bivouac, and 1300 feet above it. The greater part of the way was over a bed of snow; where there was sward, we saw wild leeks in flower, large patches of juniper, a primrose, polyanthuses, wild rhubarb, and many other beautiful flowers which we did not know.* We found a bird's nest upon the turf, with four eggs in it; the bird itself resembled a ground-lark, and was the only living creature we saw. The Leetee is formed by the melting of an immense pile of snow, which almost fills the broad glen above the fall.

Shortly after our return to our party, it began to rain and hail, but cleared up in the evening. During the night, water on the outside of the bechobas was frozen.

Bearings, &c., from the Camp.

	Bearing.	An. Elev.	Est. Dist.	Height. feet.
Pubbur waterfall	71° 30′	7° 3′	2 m. 0 f.	1296
Umrain peak, No. 1	140° 0′	36° 14′	1 m. 0 f.	3121
Umrain peak, No. 2	179° 15′	25° 12′	1 m. 0 f.	2250
Leetee waterfall	348° 30′	16° 9′	1 m. 0 f.	1469

* Juniperus squamosa? Juniper.

"We find the Rhubarb common in the Himalayas."—*Royle's Illus. Bot. Himal. Mount.* p. 315.

Temperature of the Pubbur 37° Fahrenheit.

Thermometer, highest 52°.5, lowest 34° Fahrenheit.

12th June. *Boorendo Pass,* 4 m. 4 f. elevation 15,095 feet. lat. 31° 22′ N. long. 78° 10′ E.—We left our little camp at 9 h. 25 m. A. M. The morning air was nipping and purely transparent, and from its rarity, the sky appeared of a darkling azure. Occasionally thin curling vapours issued from some of the peaks, which, I am confident, many persons at a distance might mistake for deadened volcanoes. Our track for the first two miles and three quarters passed over several remains of avalanches, and the last mile and three quarters was a continued steep ascent over a snowy slope, so steep, indeed, that a slip would have given us a most unwelcome and perhaps dangerous slide for several hundred feet. I could scarcely keep my footing upon this snowy declivity, and in hopes of greater security, pulled off my shoes. This occasioned great suffering from cold, when one of the Hill-porters, observing my dilemma, kindly gave me some grass out of his

Kiltee, and assisted me to bind it round my feet. I was very much relieved by this. However, the glistening blankness of the snow, and the rarefaction of the air, from the elevation, which made some of us experience considerable difficulty in breathing, rendered the ascent very laborious. It also hailed and snowed a part of the way, hiding the crags on each side, and sometimes even the foremost of our party: but at intervals it was clear, and we saw the glen leading to the Boorendo veiled in gloomy sublimity. It was forty minutes past mid-day when we reached the crest of the Pass, which appeared a mass of eternal snow. There were around several heaps of stones, which had been piled up by travellers, in honour of the Deotas. The Pass is flanked by two peaks covered with enormous blocks of gneiss, with their bases buried in fragments of all sizes, which have fallen, and are perpetually falling, from above.

The elevations of these two peaks have not been determined, but I estimated that on the eastward at 1000 feet, and that to the westward at 800 ft. Both peaks are so precipitous that snow only partially lies upon them. To the northward we could see the Snowy Range on the right bank of the Sutluj, which, with the one we are now upon, forms the majestic and profound glen of this river. Nine marches in a north-easterly direction from hence, is Shipkee, the frontier town of Chinese Tartary.

It snowed rather heavily for two hours after our arrival, at which time the thermometer fell to 31°.5, Fahrenheit.

The greater part of our followers had remained at the Leetee, as they did not wish to encumber themselves with carrying fire-wood up here. Those that were with us had brought but little, and were so fatigued upon reaching the Pass, from the toil of ascending, the rarity of the air, and the almost insupportable glare of the sun from the snow, which had peeled the skin from our faces, as well as theirs, that it was with much trouble we could get them to fix the Bechoba, and light a fire. When this was done, we got something to eat, and as it snowed, and the weather was hazy, and we were oppressed by the circumstances just mentioned, we kept together in the little tent, and passed the time in smoking our pipes, and trying to doze, for to sleep was impossible. We frequently heard the loosened fragments of rock, some near and some distant, rolling down with a growling noise, but fortunately none came near enough to alarm us. In this way we passed the night.

13th June, Camp at the *Leetee Torrent,* 4 m. 4 f.—Early this morning the weather became clear, and I left my fellow-travellers in the tent, and determined to climb to the summit of the western Peak, above the Pass. I experienced much labour in this attempt, as the fragments over which I clambered were but moderately firm. However I persevered, and at length stood on the top. The sky was intensely blue, and of a receding vastness. The air was stirless, cold, and oppressively pure. From here I saw the snow-clad ranges of the further Himalaya, running from N.W. to E., an assemblage, as it were, of all the mountains of the world. To the N.E. the twin peaks of the Purgkeeool, in Chinese

Tartary, rose to the skiey elevation of 22,488 feet. It was distant fifty miles. Further to the east, and about ten miles from hence, I recognised Raaldung, one of the pinnacles of the Kaaïlas, whose height is 21,103 feet, while two others, from the same mass of splintered and bare pinnacles, were 19,990 feet, and 18,068 feet. The Kaaïlas group is above a hamlet called Rispee. Seven thousand feet below me was the glen of the Sutluj, filled with a glowing blue ethereal mist, and N.N.E., at the confluence of the Buspa with this river, distant nine miles, was the village of Broang. The descent to it from the Boorendo, is by a gloomy ravine, the upper part filled with snow, the lower crowded with woods. But the object that riveted my thoughts was an immense pyramidal peak almost north, on the stupendous barrier of eternal snow beyond the Sutluj, near the Manerung Pass. It stood erect and alone in hoary majesty, like one of the superior powers of the host of white-robed pinnacles around it. The spot I was upon was a heap of decaying rocks, bound together slightly by a withered mossy soil, and a few abortive lichens. The gneiss blocks of which it was composed, were very large. These masses are, as I have already mentioned, constantly breaking away from the firmer crags, and tumbling thundering into the abysses beneath. The snowy peak, to the west of the one I was upon, was separated by a frightful chasm. It is a ghastly dislocation.

The eastern summit, above the Pass, is higher than the western, more precipitous and compact, but crumbling away, nevertheless, by the ceaseless gnawing of the frosts. The Pass itself is about fifty paces wide, strewn with the shattered rocks which have scaled from its sides. The descent from it to the Sutluj, is so steep that we did not choose to venture upon the snow-bed, which fills a part of the ravine, lest we should have had an unnecessary slide of three or four hundred yards, with the toil of re-ascending. Looking, but it was not pleasing to do so, to the south, I saw the mountains near the Choor Pahar, and had it not been for the haze in that direction, I should have seen the distant plains.

I sat down on the summit of the peak. I was alone, and how elevated! The prospect on all sides so vast, that it seemed boundless. Here, indeed, desolation, veiled in mystery, and surrounded by invisible, but dreadful ministers, reigned supreme, throned on the sepulchre of countless snow-storms. Above me was the deep splendour of the heavens, around me the winning beauty of serenitude, beneath me the all-gorgeous magnificence of the world! I felt that I was among the lowest under the glowing sapphire footstool of the Beneficent. How infinite the mind! how finite the frame! The mind infinite, for it embraced easily the vision of the earth; the frame finite, for what was I, compared with that which I beheld above, around, and beneath! The taught pride of human nature broke, and the heavenliness of humility was felt. Alas! why cannot all men smile when they pray; rejoice, when they meet; and, for the briefness of this existence, enjoy the gladness of creation? All that can make us happy has been bestowed on us, without scant or tithe, and the waters of life flow now from the cleared source. Even eternal life has been revealed from His hallowed lips! Away with the craft of worldly consecrations! Let man bow his stately form in humility to his Creator, and, in the steadfastness of confidence, trust to His paternal mercy, and rejoice in vitality!

After these reflections, I arose, and bidding farewell to that distant realm of mountains, which I should never see again, descended, slowly, to my companions.

Although the Pass is within the limit of perpetual snow on this face of the Himala, we saw several small birds about it, one of which resembled that universal favourite, the robin-redbreast,

I trust it was an excusable vanity, but I was very much pleased that I had been the first European who had ever stood on the summit of the western Peak of the Boorendo, as well as at having attained a greater elevation than Mont Blanc, besides having had a glimpse of the scarce known countries of the Northern Himala.

After breakfasting, we began our descent from

the Pass, in a manner that was novel to us, for, when the slopes of the immense beds of snow were sufficiently steep, we sat upon them, and, with a slight push, to propel us, soon dashed downwards, with immense velocity. Some of these slides were from 200 to 300 yards in length. It was quite ludicrous to see our followers whizzing, in long lines, down these white declivities, with the utmost placidity of feature. We passed, within half a mile on our left, the source of the Pubbur, which rises from the Charamaee lake, now a snow-bed. Its elevation is 13,839 feet. The stream, as I have before said, immediately precipitates itself over a ledge of rock, in a curve of a hundred feet, and is instantly buried in the snows piled along its rugged course for a mile, when it re-appears, gliding, in crystalline brightness, under arching vaults of snow. Above the lake, upon a ridge, is a massive bed of snow, at least eighty feet in thickness, which topples over, and will, eventually, fall into it. Upon the crest of the Himala, which flanks the lake, are the following passes, all close to each other.

	Elevation.
Neebrung Pass	16,035 feet
Goonnas Pass	16,026 feet
Goosool Pass	15,851 feet

Continuing our way over the snow, we passed the Moondaar Cave, a spot where travellers take shelter when crossing the Passes around. It was on our right. We soon after reached our little encampment.

Whilst upon the summit of the Boorendo we all felt, more or less, from the rarefaction of the atmosphere, fulness of the head, difficulty in breathing, pains in the eyes and ears, and headaches. I was very much affected, and scarcely dozed for two hours during the night.

The thermometer on the summit of the Pass was:—

Highest ..37°.5
Lowest....27°.5

and the temperature of boiling water 186°.5 Fahrenheit, which is 2° too much, from the known error of our thermometer,

The declivity of the Pubbur, from its source

to where it joins the Seepun, below Jangleeg, is 545 feet in the mile,

Thermometer at the Leetee torrent, highest 59°.5, lowest 35°.5, Fahrenheit.

We had showers in the evening, but it froze in the night.

14th June, *Jangleeg*.—The air was bracing and the morning lovely, which made our walk back to this place delightful, It is spring here, and exactly the spring of England. What a contrast with the season now of the plains! There the sun looks red and bloated, volumes of dust eddy over the arid soil, the wind seems to be issuing from a fiery furnace, and man sinks down exhausted and torpid with heat. But on these mountains each floweret and blade of grass before dawn bends with a dew-drop, like a novice bearing a censer; then the sun, the altar where Nature offers burnt sacrifices to JEHOVAH, rises in unveiled glory, and this pure liquid perfume, warmed by its beams, is wafted in fragrant incense to the firmament. The leaflets of the majestic cedars, oaks, chestnuts, and the delicately drooping birch, tremble with adoration, rills of fresh-born water run through the vividly green sward, and man feels that he is possessed of the nobility of reason. These magnificent Himalayan woods seem to have been created in vain. The noble trees flourish, die, and fall, often indeed across the slight path which the traveller pursues, sad emblems of dethroned majesty. Crumbling, they return to their primeval elements, and afford nourishment to another race. Their stems are frequently covered with beautiful lichens, puny parasites of timber fit for navies!

We met a number of mountaineers laden with flour, who were on their road to Koonawr, over the Boorendo. They return with salt and wool. Koonawr is celebrated for its sheep. Every thing in these elevated countries is carried upon men's backs, and it is really wonderful to see them bearing burdens from 80 to 100 lbs. across these Passes, one of which I have traversed with some difficulty even without the smallest load. It often happens, however, that on these expeditions they are frozen to death. But what will man not do for gain, enhanced by the desire of rendering those happy whom he so fondly cherishes?

During our excursions from Koteghur we have generally been able to procure goats, sheep, flour, rice, ghee or butter clarified, milk, and an abundance of excellent honey. The inhabitants seldom rear poultry. Bullocks it would be sacrilege to kill, as the Hindoo religion under some modification or other prevails. We occasionally procured fish, but the streams, for the most part, are too rapid to admit of their being easily caught.

We found, on our march this morning, the black currant, and in Koonawr, which is beyond the first snowy chain, there are gooseberries.

Thermometer, highest 65°.5, lowest 49°.5, Fahrenheit.

15th June, *Pekka,* 6 m. 2 f.—A charming walk of two hours brought us to our old encampment. The fields of Battoo and Paapur, about here and at Jangleeg, seem to promise good crops, but it is promise merely. However, much grain is not wanted where the population is so small as in the Chooaara district.*

Polyandry, as I have before observed, is frequent, and the men assigned as a reason, that their trading avocations often forcing them to be absent for a long period from their homes, it was requisite that the females should have more husbands than one. They also acknowledged that it was not uncommon to sell their children in seasons of scarcity; indeed most Asiatic nations do the same under similar circumstances, but not otherwise.

We have remarked chains, with a small bell attached to them, stretched from the store-houses to those occupied by families. This, we were informed, was to give the alarm in case of

* "In the Himalayas, Fagopyrum esculentum (phaphra and kooltoo of the natives) is also most commonly cultivated."—*Royle's Illust. Bot. Himal. Mount.* p. 317.

"Several of the Amarantaceæ, like so many of the Chenopodeæ, though without taste, are, on account of the mucilaginous nature of their leaves, used as vegetable pot-herbs, and cultivated in India; as Amarantus polygamus, polygonoides, tristis, oleraceus, gangeticus, and polystachyus. A. frumentaceus is cultivated for its seed in Mysore as A. Anardhana is in the Himalayas."—*Ibid.* p. 321.

robbery. However, I think that this precaution is only resorted to from the houses of the priests to that containing the treasure of the temple.

At Jangleeg bows and arrows were brought to us for sale, though in all the districts we have passed through, the inhabitants go about unarmed. The bows were made of bamboos, brought from the lower countries, with a string of the same material. The only bamboo I have seen here is like a tall reed. The arrows were reeds, which, when used for war, are tipped with bone. Hatchets are common; swords, spears, and matchlocks scarce. The chiefs use the latter. Feuds are frequent, and, like those of all mountaineers, cherished beyond the memory of the wrong.

Every hamlet, and indeed almost every accessible peak, has a Deota or temple, against the walls of which are nailed dogs' skulls, horns of deer, small pieces of iron, copper, and shreds of cloth. A trident, which is the emblem of Siva, the destructive Power of the Brahminical Triad, is usually fixed on the top of the roof.

Scarcity and famine are of very frequent occurrence, from the crops in these elevated districts not ripening. This is chiefly after severe winters. When this happens, the inhabitants eat venison, sheep, dried fruits, and roots.

The natives are in general a hardy and active race, and, as we have often remarked, are kind and hospitable.

Domestic cats are common.

Mortar is not used in the construction of the buildings; in fact, the only limestone I saw during the tour, was a formation of black limestone between Syree and Semla. Clay is found in small quantities, but it is not used. Mica-slate is the largest formation between the Punta Gaut, in the Tayog Purgunnah, and Pekka. Granite is scarce every where. Compact gneiss is the prevailing rock of the Parent Chain of the Himala, which being exposed to the continual vicissitudes of the weather breaks into fragments, and forms those stupendous spiry, triangular, pyramidal, and precipitous gray pinnacles, which tower above the massive ranges in barren sublimity. Amongst the lofty mountains at the base of the southern Himala, mica is found, forming rocks of enormous size and exceeding splendour. We were particularly struck with it on our way up to Jangleeg, where the slope of the valley was radiant with its fragments, like the shattered remains of some Elfin capital. Veins, and blocks of quartz and feldspar, are abundant.

The uplands in these districts are covered with a rich turfy soil. Those facing the S. E. are less precipitous, more thinly wooded, and afford finer pasture than those facing the N. and N. W., which are usually overhung with large woods, which hide their steep and torn flanks.

I have remarked no manufactures, except that of the Sooklaat, or coarse woollen cloth, already mentioned.

Thermometer; highest 78°.5, lowest 58°.5, Fahr.

16th June, *Cheergaon,* 7 m. 6 f.—We changed our route this morning, and went by one that was shorter, better, and more picturesque. Leaving Pekka, we descended 1400 feet to the Pubbur, which was wreathed with foam. At 3 m. 6 f. we passed Kundrone and Teekurree. The former is a hamlet, prettily situated, just above Teekurree; the latter a house belonging to the Rana. The path, ran occasionally along the rocky sides of the mountain, overhanging the river; but the footing, in general, was secure. The sango over the Pubbur, at Teekurree, is a very good one.

The inhabitants of Cheergaon are very busy in the poppy-fields collecting opium. The apricots are now almost ripe.

Thermometer; highest 89°, lowest 63°, Fahr.

17th June, *Rooroo*, 11 m. 2 f.—We crossed over the Pubbur by the sango at Mandlee, which is a very disagreeable one, being many feet above the tremendous torrent, and re-crossed at Rooroo by three temporary ones, over as many branches of the river. The sangos are principally unpleasant, for they are rarely dangerous, from the swaying of the spars of which they are made, and from the carelessly-arranged platform, which is nothing more than a few ill-nailed planks, covered with branches and twigs, which are prevented from being blown away by slabs of stone or slate.

In this indifferent footing are many gaps, under which the torrent may be seen, hurled like a thunderbolt.

We found this road better shaded, and pleasanter than the one I went by to the Boorendo, which was on the right bank of the river. It passed through cultivation almost the whole way.

I was informed at Rooroo that brothers usually married the same girl, and that they divided the offspring by the gentle law of primogeniture, the eldest brother taking the first-born, and so on successively. I am sorry to add, that female infanticide is also known here; but it is to be hoped, that since the British influence extends its authority over these petty states, it is of secret and rare occurrence.

Rooroo is the residence of the Chief Guru or Spiritual teacher of Bussheer. He visited us here on our way to the Boorendo, preceded by some chobdaars or mace-bearers, as a part of his ecclesiastical state, and very civilly expressed a desire to serve us, and was useful in procuring supplies of grain for our attendants. He is a fat, portly, and goodnatured man. These districts produce two kinds of rice, one peculiar to the highlands, the other to the lowlands, besides wheat and barley

We had heavy rain in the evening.

Thermometer; highest 89°, lowest 54°, Fahr.

18th June, *Kusshain*, 10 m. 4 f.—The weather cleared during the night, and we commenced our march with the thermometer at 54° Fahrenheit, and a fine morning. From the Punneeout Pass we saw the town of Sheel, on the shoulder of a mountain three miles to the left. The finest iron-ore in these districts is found at Sheel. The glens on each side of the Teekur valley, on the approach to Kusshain, are very beautiful. The Sooraar ridge closes the view. We counted twelve villages from one point of the route to-day. I also saw a large mountain dog with an immense goitre, and upon inquiry, was told that they were very subject to this glandular swelling. This, however, was the only instance that came under my own observation. Fragments of quartz strewed our path in many places during to-day's journey.

Thermometer, highest 77°, lowest 60°, Fahr.

19th June, *Sheyl*, 9 m. 4 f.—It rained again yesterday evening, and also this morning, but fortunately not whilst we were on the road. The scenery was lovely. The view, however, from the Sooraar Gaut was limited to the lower country, for in the opposite direction, although the Snowy Mountains were visible, their peaks were hid by the clouds. A few streaks only are to be seen now on the Choor Pahar. We had some fine raspberries and strawberries for our breakfast.

Thermometer highest 68°, lowest 59° Fahrenheit.

20th June, *Koteghur*, 10 m. 4 f.—Last evening it was clear and serene. This morning it rained. We marched, however, for we were anxious to see our friends, and reached Koteghur in four hours. It is a fatiguing stage. On the road we saw two flocks of sheep guarded by large Koonawree dogs, and tended by several men. Three of these dogs attacked us with great ferocity, and I believe some of us would have been bitten had I not fired at them.

CHAPTER VI.

FROM KOTEGHUR BY NAAN AND JEYTUK TO THE PLAINS.

22nd June, *Naugkunda,* 10 m. 2 f.—It was with deep regret that we left Koteghur. The short period that we had been in the mountains had given rise to feelings of such happiness that we were sad, in that they would for the future, perhaps, be but the shadows of realities! The dreams of a joyous period!

We began our march by an ascent along the made road of 2400 feet, which brought us to the Bungala on the crest of the Gaut. The route was excellent, passing amidst cedar forests interspersed with various species of fir and fine oaks. Apples, apricots, raspberries, and strawberries, were plentiful along the road. They are now ripe, but are far inferior to those of Europe.

It has rained a good deal, and we are at this place enveloped in mists. In the evening it became fine, and we saw with mingled joy and sadness, the Snowy Range extending from N. $\frac{1}{2}$ W. to E. by N. It is a magnificent prospect: the pride of the earth. A peak bearing N. and beyond the Sutluj appeared to be the loftiest of the chain. We recognised points near Sooraan and the Boorendo Pass. The immense groups of fleecy clouds which rolled thickly below our camp, gave an air of astonishing grandeur and mystery to the scene. It was so cold that we had a fire lit at night.

Thermometer at sunset 57° Fahrenheit.

23rd June, *Mutteeana,* 12 m. 6 f.—We travelled by the new road. The scenery between Naugkunda and the sango at the foot of the Gaut is very beautiful. Wartoo, which we ascended on our road to Koteghur is a long mountain, the northern extremity of which is crowned with a fort, now dismantled. The Choor Pahar is also a long mountain with a triangular pyramidal summit of green sward and gray rock. It is one of the most conspicuous of the lower hills. We were obliged to light a fire as yesterday.

24th June, *Fagoo*, 15 m.—It rained very heavily last night, but as the morning was fine, we breakfasted, and continued our journey. At Tayog we were enveloped in a thunder-storm, which drenched us to the skin, but delighted us with its sublimity. By the time we reached Fagoo the rain had ceased, and our camp-followers busied themselves in drying their clothes and cooking. We had a good view of the Boorendo and Shatool Passes in the evening. Upon looking at the Boorendo, we thought inwardly, "there have we trod, and now we are here. Is it possible that we have been there?" I know not how it was, but this simple circumstance gave rise to a most indescribable sensation. Had I, perhaps, been endowed with "metaphysics," I could have expatiated learnedly on "Idealism" and "Realism." And yet it is strange, this locomotion by the common-place act of thought.

The Choor Pahar, from the clearness of the air after the rain, appeared in all its magnificence.

There were only three snow-streaks upon it. The side nearest to us is covered with noble woods.

Fires are now our greatest comfort in the evening.

25th June, *Semla,* 11 m. 2 f.—Last night it was fine, but the morning was overcast with clouds. We started, however, at day-break, and reached Semla without rain. During the whole of the march we were, to our inexpressible regret, shrouded in thick mists, which prevented our seeing the Himala. We saw however in the course of the day Subahtoo and the Plains, but before the pulse could beat twenty, the clouds had rolled together and closed the vista. At sunset a break in the circumambient vapours disclosed a snowy peak, but alas! only for a few minutes.

At the Punta Gaut the mica-slate formation ended, and was succeeded by blue clay-slate, which continued to Mahhassoo, when it again changed to yellow clay-slate, which was the prevailing rock to Subahtoo. We lit a fire immediately upon our arrival, it was so cold.

26th June, *Syree*, 10 m. 4 f.—It did not rain last night, and the day broke fairly, but with the exception of a solitary peak, the Snowy Chain was hid in the vast ocean of surfed clouds. On the road we again saw Subahtoo and the Plains. The latter our attendants hailed with joyful acclamations, I, however, with sorrow; for I was about to bid farewell to scenes of eternal beauty, and plod wearily over heated plains, where the crimson tide of barbaric conquests had rushed, and left behind the dregs of desolation!

27th June, *Subahtoo*, 12 m. 2 f.—We had no rain on the road here. Between Syree and Subahtoo we remarked the change that told us of our approach to the Plains. The huts were thatched with straw. Buffaloes were grazing about, and we heard the howls of jackalls and the screaming of peacocks; but we shall still enjoy for some days the beauty of the mountains. This is a melancholy pleasure.

5th July. *Bauhr*, 13 m. 1 f.—We left our most hospitable and kind friends at day-break, with feelings of the greatest regret. How soon do we become attached to persons of talent and enterprise, the more so when we have been fellow-travellers with them amidst sublimity in all its forms, vast and confined, rugged and luxuriant, and always majestic! Indeed, the beauty of Nature allies sympathies of the most varied kind, with a force quite unknown to the petty and monotonous realities of every-day life.

Upon summing up my routes, I find that I have walked 370 measured miles in these mountains, exclusive of the journey to Belaspoor, during which, I partly rode and partly walked; and, as the excursion was made in the hottest months of the year, any comment upon the excellence of the climate would be superfluous.

Almost all the elevations in this Narrative, were determined, barometrically, by my very kind and experienced friend, Lieutenant Alex. Gerard, of the Bengal Infantry. The distances, also, beyond Subahtoo, were measured by him. From Subahtoo to Bauhr, the prevailing rock is clay-slate. About Bauhr earthy chlorite is abundant.

* A few of the elevations were taken from the 14th vol. of the Asiatic Researches.

6th July, *Pinjore*, 7 m. 4 f.

7th July, *Munnee Maajra*, 10 m. 4 f.—We left the Pinjore valley, and emerged on the plains.

8th July, *Ramghur*, 7 m.

9th July, *Raeepoor*, 9 m.

10th July, *Narrainghur*, 9 m.—Soon after quitting Raeepoor, we traversed the district belonging to Mahummed Jaffeer, whose ancestors had been settled there since the time of the Moghul Government. One of them, a medical man, had rendered services of importance to one of the emperors, and, as a recompense, had received these lands. The fort of Mornee was given to Mahummed Jaffeer, for assistance to our Government during the late Nepaul war. About a mile from Raeepoor we passed a large well-built fort, which belonged to him.

The first half of the road to-day was rough for wheel-carriages, and the country was covered with a low jungle. The latter half was opener, and partially cultivated. We passed through a considerable village, called Laar, and crossed the beds of three mountain torrents, with low banks.

Narrainghur belongs to Futteeh Sing, of Ulwar, in the Punjaub. He is one of Runjeet Sing's Sirdars. It is a poor fort, and was formerly in the possession of the Rajah of Sirmoor.

Naan bears N. 60° E.

11th July, *Siddowra*, 8 m.—It rained heavily last night, and inundated the country; our march to-day, therefore, was a succession of disasters, which would have been much worse, but that the soil was sandy. About half-way we crossed the Maarkoonda nullah, a broad mountain torrent, with low banks, and full of quicksands. It comes from the hills below Naan. We traversed, besides, three other streams, the last of which was, in one hour, chin-deep, and very troublesome.

Siddowra is a large town, with a good bazaar. Part of it belongs to our Government.

Naan bears N. 14° E., and we just see it peering over the hills which skirt the plains. The Choor is a majestic object from here, as is the high Seyn range, which runs between it and Jeytuk. More to the eastward we perceive what we suppose to be Baraat, and some very lofty mountains.

They also rise to a considerable height in the direction of Subahtoo.

12th July, *Naan*, 17 m., elevation 3207 feet.—Early this morning it rained heavily, but as it cleared after breakfast, we left our camp standing at Siddowra, and proceeded to Naan or Nahun. When we had gone between eight and nine miles we crossed the Maarkoonda river, and gladly entered once more into the mountains. A winding road led us to the foot of the ridge on which Naan is situated, from whence an easy, though long ascent, brought us to the town. We found our bechobas pitched on a pleasant spot, close to a house that had been built by Captain Birch, but now belonging to the Rajah.

About half a mile before reaching the town, a shed by the road-side, with a female sitting at the door of it, attracted my attention. I looked into the place and saw an infant lying on its back wrapped in a cloth, with a rillet of water falling upon its head from a small spout. It was fast asleep. I dismounted to witness, as it might be perhaps for the last time, this extraordinary custom, which is very general in the vicinity of Subahtoo, and throughout that portion of the Himala which we have visited. The woman watching the infant was its mother, and she told me that it was ill of a dysentery. About Subahtoo we often saw several infants wrapped up like little mummies and arranged in a semicircle, with small streams of water from spouts falling on their heads. They were usually watched by some elderly female, while the mothers were employed in agriculturul labours. The natives believe that it strengthens the children and renders them hardy; besides, it is the most effectual means I have ever seen of sending them to sleep. The most refractory imp, when tied up, let it yell never so loud, will, when the stream has for a few seconds bathed its head, fall into a most noiseless slumber.

We devoted the evening to the visiting of all that was interesting at Naan. The first was Lieut. Thackeray's tomb, which is on the bank of a handsome tank, called the Pukka Tallaao, in order to distinguish it, I presume, from one that is not yet faced. Poor Thackeray was killed at the siege of

Jeytuk, after performing acts of gallantry and daring, which excited the highest admiration, not only of our army, but also of the Goorka soldiery. He had, upon the forced retreat of Major Richards from his position, defended, with a small party, the retiring column against the whole body of the infuriated Goorkas, who repeatedly charged his post. At last, he was shot dead, as was Ensign Wilson. But the party was saved, and the name of their devoted preserver is as familiar to the inhabitants of this country, as that of their fathers. The most glorious conquest could not have conferred so honourable a title as that which his self-devotion has gained.*

* "The important duty of covering the retreat was undertaken by Lieutenant Thackeray, with his light company belonging to the 26th N. I. This officer's self-devotion contributed mainly to save the detachment from being entirely cut off; for, while the troops were filing down the pathway, his company kept the whole Goorka force in check, charging them several times in different directions. Its situation, of course, grew every instant more desperate; still not a man of the company thought of his individual safety, while the Lieutenant lived to command. After more than half of his men had fallen, he was himself at last killed; and Ensign Wilson, who served under him, fell nearly at the

The monument is a long slender pyramid upon a pedestal, without any inscription. There needs none. Three other graves, said to contain the remains of other fallen officers, are close to it.

We next proceeded to the Taakoor Dwara, a temple upon an eminence which commands a lovely view of the town and surrounding country. It is a small white building with a dome. Thence passing through an extensive, populous, and well-supplied bazaar, we came to the Rajah's residence, a large stone edifice upon another eminence, which, like that upon which the temple is situated, commands a rich and varied prospect. At a small distance from it are the stables, with a spacious green lawn in front, where his horses are exercised, and where, also, his troops muster.

---

same time. The covering party was then overpowered, and it was supposed at first, that the company had been cut off to a man; but it was found afterwards, that Runjoor Singh had given quarter to about forty men and a soobadar, whom he treated well; and, having vainly tempted to enlist in his ranks, dismissed a few days after, on parole not to serve again during the war."—*Prinsep's Tran. in India*, v. i. p. 101, et seq.

Turning to the north, we went to a small temple dedicated to Lutchmee Narrain. It is shaded by large peepul-trees, and charmingly situated. We concluded our walk, by going to another temple, dedicated to Mahadeo, about half a mile to the east. There are also some fine trees around it, but with the exception of the site, it is not worthy of a visit.

13th July, *Siddowra.*—It rained a little last night, and Naan was immediately enveloped in mists. It was delightfully cool, which afforded us great comfort, for we had already felt the contrast in the low country.

The plains are intolerably hot, so much so, that the system is fretted to the utmost ramification of the minutest nerve.

We arose at day-break refreshed. The morning was clear, cool, and heavenly, and we started for Jeytuk with the lightness of schoolboys going home for the holidays. The road led down the northern flank of the ridge upon which Naan is situated. The sides of the mountain are covered with underwood and trees. After a mile and a half's walk, we came to the Gusshaul river, a stream of crystalline brightness, which bounds and quivers amongst large stones and fragments of rock. We pursued the track up its bed for a considerable distance, crossing and re-crossing the current at least a dozen times. At length we quitted it, and began to climb the Jeytuk range of hills, and, after a long ascent, reached the Jumpta temple, which is on the summit of the ridge, shaded by two or three fine trees, and surrounded by bushes of jessamine. It is four miles from Naan. Here the Choor Pahar burst suddenly upon us, rearing its broad form over the lofty Sine range, between which and the spot where we stood was a deep valley. Behind us was Naan, and further, volumes of snowy and curled clouds hung over the plains.

From hence we turned eastward along the ridge for about a mile, which brought us to the fort of Jeytuk, an unsubstantial building of an oblong form, the longest sides of which are barely thirty yards in length, occupying the top of a peak. Its elevation is 4854 ft.

Between the Jumpta temple and Jeytuk we passed the ruins of two stockades, and the graves of many of the Goorkas that were killed during the siege.

We were now on the spot which in the Nepaul war had attracted the attention of all India. Here our troops had met with severe disasters; for two columns of attack had been driven headlong from this ridge. When once they were here, they should have kept the post, for the ground is excellent.

The Goorka leaders, both here and at Malown, seem to have been infatuated, for instead of fighting with us for every cartridge-breadth of ground, leading to both the forts, they concentrated their forces, and were defeated. The Jeytuk position is not so strong as the one at Malown. General Martindell's plan of attack appears to have been feasible. The surrender of Ummer Sing at Malown, included in the treaty Jeytuk and its brave commander, Runjoor Sing Tappa.

We returned from here to Naan, where we

breakfasted, and in the evening joined our camp at Siddowra. On the road I again saw at the shed the mother and her infant, and stopped to inquire if her child were better. I was pleased to hear her answer in the affirmative.

The houses at Naan are generally well built of stone, flat-roofed, and white-washed. Its situation is delightful, in the midst of fine trees. Pines, mangoes, and plantains, grow together in this enviable climate. I should remark, that Naan is the capital of Sirmoor, one of the largest mountain states between the Jumna and the Sutluj. The Rajah was at Umballa, but his officers were very courteous to us. The revenue is said to amount to 40,000 rupees, 4000*l*.

14th July, *Belaspoor*, 8 m.

15th July. Left bank of the *Jumna*, 13 m.—We are now in the Company's territory. We stopped an hour at Booreea. It is the last town of the Sikhs, situated near the old canal which formerly conducted water to Delhi. It is a large, old place, about ten miles from Belaspoor. The mango groves around it are covered with fruit. We had considerable difficulty in crossing the Jumna, which was swollen by the rains.

The hills have been hidden from us, since leaving Siddowra, by clouds. It rained heavily.

16th July, *Doonjurra*, 1 m. 5 f.—We had much trouble in crossing two nūllahs which were flooded by the rains.

In the evening the weather cleared, the legioned clouds hurried away before their aërial chief, and we once more beheld the Himalaya, serene and majestic. Jumnootree was beautiful, the very personification of sublimity, for its two peaks, joined by a snowy ridge, towered to the skies, spurning, as it were, the level of the plain, while between them a black pyramidal summit peered mysteriously, and added unceasing graces to the outline.

Some high mountains of snow, which we supposed to be those near Gungootree. bore N. E. by E. Jumnootree bears N. E.

17th July, *Chicklaana,* 1 m. 4 f.—Before daybreak the rain fell in torrents, but the evening was yet more lovely than yesterday's, and the Snowy Range yet more magnificent. Long after the deep shades were possessed of the lower mountains, those shining heights teemed with crimson-vested sun-beams, that ascended there as though to watch the world asleep. The peaks near Gungootree have a much bulkier appearance than those of Jumnootree, and one of them rises higher than any of the pinnacles that overlook the source of the Jumna.

Half lost in thought, gazing at these majestic mountains, the contrast becomes forcible. Jumnootree is the perfection of elegance, while Gungootree is vast and savage. A fit bride and bridegroom! I watched them with, may I say, an affectionate tenderness, till they were lost in the depths of evening, and to me for ever!

A LETTER

FROM THE LATE

Mr. J. G. GERARD,

DETAILING HIS

Visit to the Shatool and Boorendo Passes,

FOR THE PURPOSE OF DETERMINING

THE LINE OF PERPETUAL SNOW ON THE SOUTHERN

FACE OF THE

HIMALAYA.

NOTE

The Editor subjoins the following extract from a letter to him from Captain Alex. Gerard, relative to the last expedition of his late brother. It is painful from the loss of a friend of his childhood, but pleasing from the circumstance that he is able to pay this slight public tribute to the memory of a most enterprising traveller.

"You would be sorry to see my poor brother James's death. His trip to Bokhara with Colonel Sir A. Burnes, was a mad-like expedition for him, as he had long been unwell, and was obliged to leave his bed to go, and could only travel in a Palkee. It was however his own wish, and at his own particular request, that Burnes applied for him. This trip killed him, for he had several attacks of fever on his way to Bokhara, and Burnes again and again urged him either to return or stop at Kabool till he recovered. But he would do neither. His love of research carried him on, and he persevered and accomplished the journey with the greatest difficulty. On his return he was detained three months at Meshid, and no less than eight at Herat, by fever, so after his arrival at Soobahtoo his constitution was completely worn out. He never had a single day's good health, and gradually declined. But the doctors would not believe him on account of the florid complexion he had even on the very day of his death. Patrick and I were with him the whole time he survived, which was just a year, for I got leave of absence on purpose to prepare a map of his route from his notes; for he observed the bearings, estimated the distances, and noted the villages all the way from Herat to the Indus.

"It was a splendid map. It measures 10 feet long by 3 broad, on the scale of five miles to an inch. At my brother's dying request I presented it to Sir C. Metcalfe, then Governor-General, from whom I received a thousand thanks.

"The map is now with the Army of the Indus, and I was gratified to hear, that as far as they had gone, they had found the positions of the places and accounts of the roads wonderfully correct, considering the distances were estimated by time, and the bearings taken with a small pocket compass."

Aberdeen, October 18, 1839,

Charamaee Lake,
13,800 feet above the Sea.
18th August, 1822.

MY DEAR LLOYD,

I promised to write to you from some part of the Pabur dell; and I cannot do better than begin from the source, and if I do not entertain you I shall at least feel a pleasure in the task. As you have made the tour, your curiosity, if not satisfied, must be palled, and nothing but wonders will now please you; but the field has yet its interest to one who is alive to its beauties and grandeur. I am here only two months later than you were, but what a change! the snow indeed lies all around here at the lake and below in the dell, covering the Pabur over in many places, but the sides of the mountains are free, and green sward is spread over them to an almost incredible height. In June the whole was sheeted in snow, and I believe you made but one step from Boorendo Pass to the bed of the Pabur, and now scarce a patch remains of what must have appeared to you quite indestructible; such is the effect of the moist warmth of the rainy season. I had expected this, and I am peculiarly glad at having come here at the proper time to verify the fact, since to you and other travellers who are obliged to take the advantage of the most favourable period for such a journey, the appearances now exhibited are likely to be entirely at variance with the conclusions that you would naturally have formed from the state of the climate and country at the Summer Solstice. I got up here about two hours ago, having made your march, only my camp was on the left bank of the river which I crossed by the Snow. I know not what came over me to-day, but I reached this with the utmost difficulty, being quite overpowered before I arrived at the Cliff of the Cascade. My intention was to have pitched on the ridge above this, which is 16,000 feet, and is crossed by the passes to the Buspa Valley, but had there been a gold-mine on the top I could not have made the attempt. This was the only time I felt exhausted to such a degree, although often exposed to severer fatigue at far greater elevations. You know the ground as well as myself, the only ascent being the gradual rise of the river, which to the rock of the lake does not exceed 500 feet per mile. This is the most remarkable instance of the effect of a cause not clearly understood, that I have yet experienced, but I shall not tire you by a theoretical discussion, but rather tell you of my adventures, and however deficient in interest the narrative, if it only makes you look back upon your trip with half the pleasure that I derived from your visit, my object will be attained. I left Subaḥtoo on the first, and slept at Nagkhanda the same night. Arrived all wet to an empty house, bad management you will say, within eight miles of Kotgurh. On the 2nd I went on to Shyl, your stage, taking Wartoo in my way, where I observed the barometer at 20.535, temperature of the open air 57°. This was a dreadful day, the rain pouring down in torrents; and sinking to the knee at every step, my spirits here began to fail me when I saw my miserable camp lingering in the mud, my people sick, some deserting, others abjuring their promise to go on. The morning came as if nothing had preceded it, and looking at the calm face of nature I forgot my troubles, and wondered at my inconsistency. By 10 o'clock I was in the Suroor Pass, 9,700 feet. The view was confused by a mist, but I could see a few white tops through it. I stopped at Kushaen, a stage of yours. The climate here was warmer than I expected to find it from the elevation of 7000 feet. Thermometer rising to 79° in the afternoon. This day was fair. On the fourth I reached Rooroo, where the air felt sultry and uncomfortable. The sun shone out his course, and the temperature rose to 85°, but the margin of the river was agreeable. The stream was not so full as the season of the year led me to anticipate; a fair day makes a vast difference here where the water runs off as fast as it is fed by the rain. At some period of July the river must have risen to a great swell, for torrents that had been brim full were now dry, the only traces of their size and force being the destruction to the fields. The Pabur is still a fine stream when we bring the scenery into the picture, but by itself it may be compared to the sea without a ship. The young rice had shot up, and the plantain-trees and the Mimosa told me I was still in a tropical climate, yet who could imagine that in four days' travelling we are already amongst perpetual ice, with darkness and desolation all around, and that a stream of this size should so soon degenerate into a rill, and close itself in the drippings from the snow? On the 5th I was in the neighbourhood of mountains, on whose sides some patches of snow still remained, but their summits are uncovered at this season. It had rained in the afternoon, and in the evening I had a sight of the Hans Bussun, now quite black and dreary. It had lost all its snow, and we would say its grandeur, but the dark solitary aspect of its mass was not without its interest to one who made a journey for the sight; I think it is 17,500 feet, an astonishing height in this parallel of latitude to conceive that it does not enter the region of perennial showers of snow, and concluding from the state of the climate in the lower zones of the atmosphere, we should infer, that the clouds at those vast heights either appeared in the form of dew, or deposited rime at this season. I was here myself at an elevation of 8500 feet in a temperature of 60°, the thermometer exposed in the rain, which clearly showed that the anomaly was only to be explained on the greater developement of heat in the interior of the mountains, or in other words that the seasons of the country in the vicinity of the Himalaya Chain, do not correspond to those nearer the plains. Your own tour must have made this apparent, but this is a dry subject, and will do better for a magazine. On the 6th I arrived at Rol, the highest village in the Andretee Dell, and the last one in this direction. The march was fatiguing, although short. The road bad, and in the bed of the stream tangled by long grass. The bridge is a fallen fir-tree, and requires some address and activity to get safe over. The height of Rol is 9400 feet, the same as Jangleeg, and is also situate in a recess of the mountains, but perched on a jut of the great range between the forks of the Andretee, full on a southern exposure, and less circumscribed in that direction by hills, is warmer. The season had pressed less severely than I was led to expect, from the backward state of the crops in June, but the people were gathering in the Chamaas, which you know is a wild root; but I observe is not so much used as a necessary substitute for grain as for a relish, and the indolent habits of the people would incline them to the choice of a spontaneous production rather than to the cultivation of the soil.

I now made preparations for ascending the parent chain, and I may say, to take leave of the world for some time, and I could not but wonder at the facility of the change, and rapidity of my movements, which, in six days, carried me from the threshold of the plains to regions of everlasting snow, and this, too, at the worst season of the year; so much for my resolution and good fortune. The climate, at this elevation, was by no means cold, the thermometer, in the rain, varying from 58° to 59°, and when the sun beamed for a few minutes, it rose to 71°, which confirmed what I had long suspected, that the clear months of May and June are not midsummer here. On the 7th, at nine o'clock, I began the ascent, passing through the usual forest-belt that vegetates on the slopes of the main range. By noon, I halted in a cave at the height of 12,000 ft., a little above the boundary of the trees. A dense mist hid every thing around: we were in the body of the cloud, which, at this zone, descends "en masse," and we were soon covered with rain like hoar-frost. After regaling myself with segars, I continued my course, descending into a gorge, where lay a broken arch of snow over a torrent, that forced a passage in a dark worn rift, but no sooner saw the light of day, than it was precipitated under the snow. These chasms are crossed with some difficulty and agitation. Every where they represent the work of ages past, and destruction to come; and the streams tear their course with a noise as if they would swallow the whole earth up. We were enveloped in thick mist and thicker rain the rest of the way, and, although on a general level of between 12,000 and 13,000 ft., the temperature of the rain was 53°;

and when the sun peeped out, we felt a glow of damp heat, that reminded us of a better climate. In the afternoon, we halted at a cave in the trough of a torrent, which rushed past it with force and foam. These woodars, or resting-places for travellers, are but poor places of accommodation. They are most frequently formed by a ledge of rock, having a greater or less inclination beyond their base, and open to the rain on every stir of the wind. They answer very well for the inhabitants of these upland climes, who wear the fleece in every temperature, but are ill-suited for the sojourners of the plains, who, to speak emphatically, I should say, were all face, or literally uncovered. The elevation of the camp was close upon 13,000 ft., and the tent was pitched amongst a profusion of plants; and I almost sighed on being obliged to pluck up the yellow cowslip, the water lily, polyanthus, and many others, to make room for the barometer. They gave me much trouble. Rank in blossom, and spreading their roots in a soft spongy soil, I could never approach them, even on my knees, to make an observation, but they nodded, and the barometer was often nearly upset. They were the flowers of the wilderness, born to blush and fade unseen. I was here beyond the limit of forest. The junipers had even ceased to grow, but they were a very little lower, and afforded us fuel for fire. It rained incessantly day and night, but the temperature was generally from 49° to 50°, and never under 47°. Being confined to the tent, I had little else to think of, but the opportunity I had of verifying or disproving my conjectures on the climate of the great range, at a period when it undergoes a change as rapid as it is wonderful, as if an effort to break through the protracted torpor of a nine-months' winter. I was never before here in August, and I had now to decide points where frost no longer chills the air; where plants flourish, fade, and vanish; where the snow takes possession of the sides and summits of the mountains, and fresh falls sprinkle the surface; limits which have not yet been fixed in this parallel of latitude. My stop here was conclusive, and I no longer wondered at the sudden disappearance of the snow from the contiguous tracts, or the black summits of the loftiest peaks. On the 8th, the rain continued, and I became quite impatient to get to higher ground, wishing rather to be blocked up at the pass itself, where solitude and restraint have more interest. At 5 o'clock of the afternoon the rain ceased, and I struck the tent and took a course straight up the slope of the mountains for three-quarters of a mile, and at sun-set encamped on a turfy spot, where the barometer was 18.135, corresponding to an elevation of almost 14,000 feet, but the grass only began to break up, and plants were still in vigour here and there. Insulated masses of rock appeared, and far below this, slips of loose fragments laid bare by torrents of liquid snow, crossed the verdant slope. But these occur in every region of the mountains, and are owing more to the configuration of their masses, than any effect of a rigorous climate. The night was fine, the clouds having settled in the dell below. The thermometer was 44°, and I sat by a large fire in the open air, looking at the stars, which flashed with great brilliancy in so pure an atmosphere. In such a situation, solitude may be compared to Milton's "darkness visible."

The idea that we are beyond the habitable world makes us catch eagerly the stir of the wind, the flutter of an insect, or the noise of some rock in its fall; and although we feel an emotion that we cannot describe, the mind still partakes of the serenity of the region around. The morning of the 9th was fine, but fogs were rolling about at the feet of the mountains, and a light haze obscured the sky. Thermometer 45°. I was up early, it being my intention to remove my camp to the Shatool Pass. Around the tent, vegetation was still thick, and where there was moisture, luxuriant; but the continuity was broken by pieces of rock, and the soil more sparingly covered. One cake of snow, a few yards square, rested in a hollow, but it was almost eaten through, and could not hold together beyond a few days. The watercourses were already dried up, being fed by the snow, which no longer existed. All this I had fully anticipated, notwithstanding the horrid aspect of the country in June, and I felt pleasure in recording the fact, that at a height of 14,000 feet, the sloping sides of the mountains, looking to the east and south-east, were entirely free of snow, and still productive; and in the vicinity of streams or thawing snow, at great elevations, the most beautiful flowers started up. My breakfast arrived from the cave very late, the whole camp having been left below. After a hurried repast, and seeing every body on the road to the Pass, I continued ascending the same slope, in prosecution of my object, amongst rock and verdure mixed. As it required some exertion to get on at this height, I amused myself gathering flowers, which were still plentiful. At 11 o'clock I felt tired, and took an observation of the barometer, which indicated a height of 14,500 feet. Much rock was now exposed, but only where steep, and in the chinks where water had collected, were tribes of flowers, although of few varieties. I found it often impossible to trace the end of their migrations and commencement of new ones, but I could always determine the height beyond which they occurred. Passing over cairns of loose stones, and ledges as smooth as a looking-glass, I came to a group of plants of many colours, in a recess, watered by springs oozing from fissures in the rock, an oasis in a desert; all around being taken possession of by the bare rock, and beyond this, to the top, a perfect wreck. It was noon when I got up, and the clouds were rolling up the sides of the hills; I made all haste to get an observation of the barometer. When adjusted, it stood at 17.440 inches, answering to an elevation of 15,000 feet. We were in a thick fog, but even here the air felt mild, and although the sun was only visible through the mist, the thermometer was 56°. Not a patch of snow was met with in any part of the ascent, and only a stripe or two lay near our path, which would melt away in a few days. I could go no further in this direction. A mural precipice formed a horrid chasm to the west of us, which was flanked by a still loftier ridge beyond it: perpetual snow lay in the gap: the head grows giddy, and the eyes dim, at the sight;

never was ruin more complete, or confusion more confounded. I waited for some time to get the direction of the pass, hoping to reach it by continuing on the ridge we were now upon, the great object being to preserve the level; but we could only now and then get a sight of the near cliffs. At last we discovered under us, through the mist, a sloping plane, chequered with stripes of snow and black turf, apparently 600 feet below us. The effect was beyond description, for we no sooner beheld it than the mist closed in, and it vanished from our sight, and had we not verified our ideas of its reality, it might have passed for an optical delusion, or what we know, by the "Fata Morgana." Flushed with the prospects of bringing our toils to an early conclusion, we approached to the edge of a line of rocks that bordered on the plain, but what was our surprise on finding that we durst not make another step, so dense was the mist. We had come to a *ne plus ultra*, without knowing it. We turned horrified from the sight. Unwilling to retrace our steps, we made many a track in search of a break by which to descend, but none of the passages offered any chance of success, and often after getting over a difficult part into a rift, we were stopped by a cliff front. Tired of reverses, we sat down, and removing the largest stones in our power, we contented ourselves in the effects they produced. Still we had hope in discovering a gorge that would bring us to the plain, but they defied all our efforts, and only showed us the path from time to eternity. We kept along the edge of the barrier, which was crowned by a wall of snow, ten feet high, and had just receded enough to leave a narrow space of soil between it and the precipice. The snow was thawing fast, and where a stream had scattered itself, we found a species of crocus, violets, and cowslips, all full blown. They formed a carpet of many colours, at a height of 14,500 feet. We ran along the brink of the declivity and raised a flock of birds (golden pheasants), but they were shy, and fled our approach. These are the birds, I imagine, which were taken by Fraser for grouse, and the young ones bear a great resemblance to them. Here we were fortunate in finding a break which led into the plain. It was formed by the crumbling away of the rocks, but the cliff was so frail and rugged, that when it separates from its hold, the passage will be blocked up. By this we descended. In the plain the barometer was 18.100, equal to a height of 14,000 feet; a misty rime fell upon us, as the thermometer was 52°, and the air felt warm. The snow had almost all melted away, and exposed a soft black turf, which extended for some hundred yards in a dead level, and was crossed by innumerable watercourses, now dry. I have been here in July, when they were full, and if one could shut out from the scene the surrounding ruin and perpetual winter of the peaks, we might transport our imagination to the heaths of Scotland. Although the sod was still moist, yet, owing to the flatness of the spot, the snow had but recently left it, and the vegetation, which was now only bursting forth into light, would be checked by the return of winter before it had half evolved; but around us were green knolls, swelling up to 500 feet higher, then softening into another plain (the one looked down upon from the peak), where the snow lay in broad ribands, above which, the shoulder of a mass now and then reared itself, still speckled with green sward and stripes of snow. From this lofty level rose the rock of the detached summits, where no living thing was to be seen. It is quite impossible to convey, by the medium of language, the impressions excited by the contrast of such objects, but the effect is chiefly to be traced to ideas formed beforehand. Our situation at the threshold of the tropics, between India and Tartary, the sultry climate and thickened horizon of the one, the rigorous and brilliant sky of the other; then the positive knowledge of our own elevation, without all of which the perpetual snow and masses of the cliffs would cease to wear that desolate grandeur. The mind must follow in the scene, and connect itself with the objects, to complete the picture. Soon after leaving the plain we found ourselves amongst a jumble of ruins, where a little address and agility were necessary for our safety; and descending still further, we came to the slope of the mountains that form the pass. Our elevation was now 13,500 feet, so that we were 1500 feet further from the crest than before, hence the exertions we made to get into the first plain. Our prospects were dreary enough on finding the level so low, for, already worn out, we had the most arduous part to perform. The snow lay here in enormous bodies, extending, unbroken, along the ravine which drains off the waters from the pass. Much of the snow is detached from the cliffs into the dell below, which is locked in on every side; here it melts very rapidly, and the drippings, together with currents from loftier beds, generate a very considerable stream, even at its source; but such is the extent of the mass, that winter returns before it is half dissolved. In drawing the boundary of the eternal snow, we cannot bring it to so low a level, or we must cut off the fine plains of turf and flowery verdure which extend beyond it; this would be proving an absurdity, since, with equal correctness, we might limit the phenomena to the region of flourishing woods of hoary oak, pine, and rhododendron, where accumulations of snow stand out the whole year round. I rested here half an hour, and felt no inclination to quit the spot. On one hand I beheld a sward, on the other scabrous cliffs, sheeted with ice on their tops; their sides desolate; at their feet ruin, and in the middle, a valley of snow. In the spring, when the sun begins to have power over the mass of snow, it separates, and bears down all the loose pieces of rock in its way, and the whole settling from the gradual thawing of the under stratum, the rocks are left naked, and look like "islets" in the ocean. We made very slow progress over the snow to the height of 13,800 feet, where it was broken up by the steep face of the mountains. Vegetation now put forth its fullest beauty, as if in trophy of a victory of animate over inanimate nature. I much regretted the want of a portable barometer, for it was now raining, and the wind blew hard, and prevented me using the one I had, which you know requires several adjustments, and takes some time to get ready in such a situation. One cannot be better employed in the worst of circumstances; moving becomes an effort, and the necessity of stopping to breathe, offers many opportunities that we should lose, if nothing interfered to delay us. In the midst of every thing disagreeable, it rained harder, and the cold increased with the ascent, but we could not quicken our progress. We saw the tent in the pass, and people moving about on the ridge, apparently close to us, but we were always deceived. At about the height of 14,700 feet, as judged by the site of a former camp, a mass of snow crossed the road, and by its slow dissolution, had spread round it many flowers, but the rock was every where visible. Here was a plant like a full-grown cabbage, and although we find it vegetating far below this level, it did not seem to contract till it was exterminated altogether. The want of soil, more than the rigours of the climate, limits the zone of the vegetable tribes. Beyond this there was no continuity, although slips of verdure might still be traced to the height of 15,000 feet, where soil had gathered, and it was owing to the ruins of peaks, extending in all directions, that the line was not well defined. The wind blew furiously as I approached the crest, and the rain by this time had soaked us quite through; but there was no getting over our troubles sooner, had our safety depended on it. The smallest attempt to make an effort threw us back. The extreme labour we had in getting up the last 500 feet cannot be described. Anxiety and slight sickness deprived us of using our arms when inclined to break off a chip of rock by the blow of a hammer; respiration was free, but *insufficient*: our limbs could scarcely support us, and the features collapsed as if precursors of a fever. Long fasting, previous fatigue, and eagerness in the object of my tour, altogether may have had some effect in regard to myself; but the people who attended me, young, active, and robust, selected for the purpose, and having nothing to burden them, were so far in the rear, that had I wished to make a barometrical observation I must have waited a quarter of an hour. They were even more helpless than myself. On getting up I was surprised to find the thermometer in the rain at

46°. We were at an elevation of more than 15,500 feet. The rain was very light; here more like rime. This is always the case in those regions that are beyond the lower boundary of the clouds; and, as we diminish the thickness of the stratum, by ascending higher and higher, we arrive at vapour, which gradually expands till the air can no longer support it; but this occurs at a far loftier region than the theorists have assigned to it, for we find the summits of more than 5½ miles in perpendicular height loaded with snow. I found the tent pitched on the west side of the Pass, 15 feet above it. The people in a miserable condition, but with their usual provoking submission, they sat exposed to wind and rain rather than make any exertion to kindle a fire. I lost my temper, but I received a lesson which I shall never forget, and I have no doubt that one of a fuller habit of body would sink under the effects of apoplectic suffusion. The blood forsakes the extremities, and the pressure on the surface being so much diminished under the thin air, rushes into the head and produces giddiness. I felt cold and uncomfortable, and determined to take a dram, but I was treated with vinegar, the only liquor brought from Rol. I therefore put up the barometer, and went to bed at 5 o'clock. You who have passed a night at 15,000 feet know what it is, but you do not know all. A party may enjoy the absolute misery of a change, and each derive some satisfaction from the misfortunes of the other, when all are equally wretched; but the scene has no such charms to a solitary traveller, and no familiar tongue echoes back the lamentation. At sunset it faired for a few minutes, and the thermometer was 41°, but the rain began again, and the wind rose. As many of the people as could find room were sheltered in the tent, and the night came worse than the day. It blew with unusual force, and the tent creaked like an old basket. I suffered from head-ache, and every one had some complaint. At 9 o'clock a dreadful crash took place. It was like a burst of the loudest thunder over our heads, and for some time it was doubtful that we had escaped, till we caught the hollow sound of a mass of snow that had broken loose and slipped into the dell. I smoked segars but had no appetite for food. About midnight another avalanche occurred, so near to us that we apprehended it was only the first crumbling of a large mass at the foot of which we are. Morning came without misfortune. A light sky was over us, and a haze flitted about the peaks. The thermometer in the open air 37°. A thin crust of ice had formed on pools in the snow, but the tent was dripping and the ground quite moist. The rain had driven away the frost that would otherwise have settled. The adjoining cliffs, which on the east rise to 1500 feet higher, showed no appearance of new snow, but on others, where the snow was eternal, a fresh sprinking was visible at a height of 16,500 feet, while those that were very steep, and had lost their snow early in the season, exhibited their black sides to the height of 17,000 feet.

Thus far, the desiderata respecting the climate of the lofty regions of the air, that rests upon the Himalaya, were resolved, and they will serve to illustrate my speculative opinion on the height of the great Tartaric Chain which I have more than ever reason to believe exceeds 29,000 feet. My observations here furnish the following conclusions :—

1st. That July and August are Midsummer in those regions where at heights of 15,500 feet it rains during the 24 hours, but under a clear sky the air is frosty, and ice forms on standing water.

2nd. That summits of 16,500 and even 17,000 feet do not always present the phenomena of fresh snow, but on the prevalence of long-continued rainy weather or high wind, they are sprinkled: this vanishes in half an hour of sunshine, from which it appears that the Isothermal lines are positively on the same level in the Himalaya and Tartaric mountains: for in July the new snow descends to 16,500 feet in the vicinity of the table-land. This fact is at variance with the late opinion of the "Quarterly Reviewer," who to give an explanation of an anomaly that he does not comprehend, infers the superior temperature of the interior mountains; while the reverse exists, since it freezes in Tartary at a lower elevation than on the Indian side of the Himalayan Chain, and snows at the same level.

The morning of the 10th was fine, south-eastward the clouds rested on the sides of the Chang-seel Range, which you know stretches out from the Source of the Pabur in a line of rocky cliffs, but softens into a table-land, which is continuous beyond sight. It was green to the top, and had a most imposing portraiture. Rising above the belt of cloud it seemed to enter a region of perpetual vapour. Northward Trans-Sutluj the peaks were quite white, and the dell was filled up with clouds, which rolling about, assumed a thousand forms with incredible velocity. The day promising well, I made an excursion to the cave on the north side of the pass, where in September 1820 I made my ill-resolved attempt to cross. At the height of 14,800 feet we found the bones and clothes of the Brahmin who carried a bundle of sticks. What could have made this unfortunate wanderer miss the cave, and come on here alone? He no doubt became drowsy from the cold, and like the man in the fable called on death to relieve him of his load.

The bundle of sticks lay beside him. Four hundred feet lower lay the skeleton of another body (likely the same that Sandy saw in 1817, with all his clothing on, and his corpse untouched.) Below this we came upon the body of the little boy who carried the field-book and all the papers of the route. He was half buried under the snow. He lies at 13,500 feet. We searched in vain for traces of the books, so that they are for ever lost. This being a chief object of my tour, and one I had much at heart, it made me look forward to the rest of it with less interest, but I had determined to ascertain the correct elevation of the cave, and continued descending. The dell on this side is open, the hills apart, and the stream spreads over a fine level. Enormous bodies of snow, that had been detached from the neighbouring mountains, extended across the dell, covering the stream, and uniting both sides by a band. Vegetation was poor and scattered, although we were at 13,000 feet. The cliffs are scabrous and inaccessible, and are crumbling away very fast. The cave is formed by the contact of two enormous blocks of feldspar, which with a thousand others form part of an avalanche, and the break from which they were hurled looks so rugged, that one constantly expects to be annihilated, The barometer was here 18.900, answering to an elevation of nearly 12,800 feet, but the climate was mild, the thermometer rising to 64°, and at daybreak 48°. Yet so early as the 24th September it snowed very hard all day. Owing to my usual bad arrangements, I was here again very uncomfortably situated, with nothing to eat or drink. Surely, I thought, there was some curse attached to this cave, and the more I considered the misfortunes attending my adventure, the more I wondered at my folly, or rather the impulse which determined so rash an attempt. The details of that tour embraced a vast field of observation in tracts unvisited by Europeans, and at the close of the journey I was deprived of the whole. I felt symptoms of head-ache in the descent, and they did not leave me till the afternoon. I went out to gather flowers, but was obliged to return. I awoke at daybreak unrelieved by sleep, and made the best of my way towards the pass. The same sensations of debility and languor were felt on the ascent as before, but were less severe, and I did not arrive till near 10 o'clock.

Of the pass itself, and the climate, together with my own situation, I shall give you a short description, believing that it will be acceptable, although without novelty to one who has been at the source of the Pabur. To others, I should be inclined to confine myself to the wonders of the scenery, but this would only suit those who prefer being entertained by incident to being instructed by facts.

The whole period of my halt here was four days, and I might say, I reposed in the clouds, for the sun was scarcely ever visible, except on the day I came up from the cave, when he shone with an ardour that astonished me, and an hour's exposure would have made my face a fine memento of his power even here. At 10 o'clock the thermometer, screened from the wind and the sun's rays, rose to 65°, on the edge of the great field of eternal snow, the radiation from which was intolerable to the eyes. The temperature of the wind at the same time was 52°. This developement of heat, at a time when we should suppose that little or none could be derived from an atmosphere perpetually obscured, is the more surprising, since in the middle of June, a period when the sun commonly shines out his course, the temperature seldom rises to 40°, and during the night it falls to 24°, and a keen frost takes place. Your trip to the Boorendo Pass exhibits the rude climate of June, at a height of 15,000 feet; and as this is the warmest season in the plains, would be apt to mislead the unexperienced, who would infer that the subsequent months of July and August brought back snowy weather; but, see the contrary! At noon of this day, the usual fogs and rain returned, thermometer varying in it from 44° to 45°. At 5 o'clock it cleared away, and the evening set in frosty. Thermometer at sun-set 40°, and at 10 o'clock 39°, heavy dew falling; night calm and brilliant, the stars raying with great beauty. The morning of the 12th was foggy, and the frost had been driven away; thermometer 41°. We were soon in rain clouds and a high wind, and before 11 o'clock new snow appeared within 500 feet of the pass. It then sleeted, and finally turned to snow, which fell very thick. The thermometer had gradually sunk to 37°; none lay on the rocks at this elevation, but the eternal snow at the back of the pass was lightly sprinkled. At 500 feet above this the peaks were hoary, and all beyond this white. I did not expect this, although I was assured by the villagers of the occurrence, who also told me, that on the prevalence of a high wind and dark weather, the snow sometimes lay a few inches deep in the crest, and the delight with which they now saw their assertion verified, was held up as a test of the good faith and sincerity of their professions; and they claimed a present of tobacco on the occasion. I intended to have moved my camp to-day, but it rained and sleeted all afternoon. Much rock and snow have separated from their hold, and been precipitated below. Flocks of birds kept hovering over us, as if the harbingers of approaching winter. They even came and perched on the tent-ropes; and I am almost certain that I recognised the robin red-breast. At what period the snow again begins to descend below this height, I shall not have an opportunity of deciding, but I suppose not till the end of the month; and although Mr. Moorcroft was in a thick snow on the 30th of this month below the Neetee Pass, still it does not appear that there is any general change in the climate till the beginning of September; and by the end of that month hard frosts prevail, and fresh snow descends under the limit of forest. To-day's observation establishes the fact of snow-showers in the middle of summer, at the height of 15,500 feet, and as it actually drifted considerably lower, we may fix this line at 15,000 feet; but the snow does not find a resting-place, except under very unusual circumstances, and only at 16,000 feet sprinkles the mountains. Now Mr. Moorcroft had his tent covered two inches deep when close to Mansarowur, and on the surface of the ground it lay in greater quantities; and if his elevation was 17,000, we have clear evidence that the climate of the table-land, notwithstanding the increased heat from the reverberation of a bright sun, is equally as cold as in the regions of eternal snow in the Himalayan chain, although the country of the former exhibits no perpetual snow, except at heights of 18,000 and 19,000 feet. My visit here has removed the doubt I had respecting the phenomena of new snow in the passes in July and August, and I have little reason now to discredit the singular accounts of the people who live at the foot of the mountains, on the accidents which sometimes happen to travellers in crossing. They say that one year, in this month, four people perished at their night's resting-place under the pass; and they indeed assert, that the disposition to drowsiness and debility is most to be apprehended in the rainy season, and traders who are so unfortunate as to be caught in a snow-shower, or, when wet through, are exposed to the wind, often fall into a sleep, from which they never awake. The cause here is not quite obvious, nor are those extraordinary symptoms of prostration of strength, anxiety, and mental imbecility satisfactorily explained, and while we cannot hesitate to refer the primary and immediate agent to the thinness of the air, or more properly, the diminished pressure, by which the balance of the circulation is destroyed; nevertheles , the effects are so capricious and irregular, as to be at variance with the idea of a constant cause, which leads many to disbelieve the existence of even any one symptom, and those who have by accident resisted the impression in crossing the mountains, remain unalterable in their conviction; but I know that you will give me credit for what I relate, although you only experienced head-ache in the Boorendo. I also have passed the night there free of every symptom, unless weakness on making an effort. The people who live at the foot of the mountains, and who either breathe a highly-rarefied air, or are accustomed to ascend their steep sides, suffer much less than those who inhabit a lower zone and denser atmosphere; but they are well acquainted with the effects, and describe their feelings with an ingenuous simplicity, which is highly interesting. It is astonishing to see what enterprise and necessity will accomplish in the rudest state of society. Between Koonawur (where people seem born to live and die in the bosom of inaccessible barriers), and the Indian side of the mountains, we find a very extensive intercourse by the crest of the mountains, at a positive elevation of 16,000 feet: I met crowds of people daily, laden with grain, and although they made slow progress, often halting to breathe. yet they seemed to labour under an uniform oppression. I have not learnt whether they are subject to occasional indisposition, such as that I experienced, however this may be, it is indisputable that, beyond a certain height, the effects of the rarefied air upon the functions of animal life are permanent, and neither custom nor constitution can bear up against them. Sandy and I, in our excursion to the peak, of 19,500 feet, although unable to take a dozen of steps without being exhausted, and latterly could scarcely move at all, nevertheless outdid the villagers, who accompanied us, and reside at the height of 12,000 feet. In the interior of the country, where the soil is remarkably elevated, the most dreadful symptoms are felt in crossing the mountains. Between Ladak and Yarkund, I have been told by an intelligent servant of Mr. Moorcroft's, of fatal consequences from the want of due precaution. He says that the passage of the lofty range should be made while fasting, and recommends frequent doses of emetic tartar during the journey. He relates an instance of a wealthy Russian merchant who was on his way to Leh, of Ladak, to see Mr. Moorcroft, having perished in crossing one of the passes because he made a hearty meal before starting. Death, in such a case, may be more properly attributed to somnolency, brought on by cold and the extreme rarity of the air, which predisposes to inactivity, that fascinates the helpless traveller into his last long sleep As respiration cannot be performed in a vacuum, we should consider that, at the height of 18,480 feet, the exhaustion is already half made, and, as the whole can only have effect through the agency of its component parts, the progressive action becomes here an arithmetical series, reducible to an experiment in natural philosophy, where each succeeding stroke of the piston of an air-pump appears to draw the hand placed on the aperture closer and closer, till the pressure above so much overbalances that below, as to be insupportable to the person without risk of detriment. At 18,480 feet, the barometer, in the mean state of the air, stands at 15 inches, so that here we breathe an atmosphere half the density of that at the level of the sea; how then can we be surprised at the effects? I hope I have made myself clear on this subject, and I now return to the Shatool.

The weather was unfavourable for research, and, with the exception of my trip to the cave, I scarcely left the tent. I had made up my mind to attempt to reach the top of Hans Bussun, or a peak very like it, which I was struck with in returning from the cave. The approach seemed easy over the snow to within a few hundred feet of it, but I had no opportunity—I afterwards found out that I had mistaken another pinnacle for the Hans. However, it was a mass rising to 17,000 feet, and I felt a great desire to seat myself on its summit, not so much on account of the actual elevation, as to be insulated in the Snowy Chain. I could then have pointed to my station from Wartoo, and said to *travellers* in their noviciate, "Go there and behold the wonders of the world!" The afternoon of the 12th was rainy, and the new snow disappeared to the height of 16,200 feet. The evening was fine, thermometer 39° at sun-set, and ice forming over the perpetual snow. I took a walk for a short way up the rocks, to get a better view of the neighbouring country, but the sensation of fulness in my head obliged me to return. Since my arrival here I was more or less affected by head-ache, which has been most troublesome at night; the pain is not like that of a common head-ache, but as if a dead weight was attached to all sides of the head, at once pulling in contrary directions. I have found great relief from tea, but it was only temporary; thus the pleasures we contemplate from an abode in these elevated regions, is almost destroyed by the same cause which excites so much interest in the adventure. One will even court the hardships of climate and country, if, at the end of his toils, he is greeted by the object of his search, and can survey it without an effort; but here we labour for a possession which we cannot enjoy. The scene is therefore of unapproachable grandeur. The morning of the 13th was foggy, thermometer 38°.5; no frost; the night was a dreadful one of wind and rain, and I suffered much from head-ache, which passed into drowsiness, similar to the sedative effect of intoxication. I have never experienced so decided a proof of the existence of an agent inimical to the principles of animal life, for although I suffered much more in Boorendo Pass, in 1818, yet it was not kept up day after day, as it has been here. All my people have also been affected in different ways, some with sickness, others with head-ache; but because every one is not equally affected, we are not to infer that chance has brought it about; we might as well say, that the natural conditions of energy and action are always the same.

The extremes of the barometer were here 17.055 and 17.160 inches, the attached thermometer 41°.5 and 53°, at these periods, and the main temperature of the climate 42°, which, from corresponding observations at Koteghur and Soobahtoo respectively, 6660 and 4205 feet, will give 15,500 feet for the height of Shatool Pass above the sea, which is 200 feet lower than Humboldt's equatorial limit of perpetual snow, as it occurs on teh flanks of Chimborazo. I shall not stop to inquire what phenomena have been attended to in the determination of this point, but only observe that the line in the latitude 30° 30′, in Asia is fixable at 15,000 feet on the southern or Indian aspect of the Himalaya mountains, and on the northern (not the Tartaric) may be concluded at 14,500 feet; but there are so many conflicting conditions of the question, that no precise boundary can be assigned without an explanation.

The place of encampment was here not only free of snow, but was enlivened by plants of the cryptogamous lichen family, which vegetate at 500 feet higher, or 16,000 feet of absolute elevation, where patches of soil are still met with. I have ascended to this height, which is the summit of the peak that flanks the pass on the west. Beyond this is a chasm, and then another mass, or rather a group of hoary tops, between 17,000 and 17,500 feet. The Hans Bussun is the last pinnacle of the chain before it is broken by the Sutluj, and could not have been more than five miles from me, but it was not visible from this neighbourhood. The cheeks of the pass are perfectly naked long before this time of the year, and the trough formed by them, although sheeted with snow at the summer solstice, is now bare rock down to the ravine on the south side, with the exception of some accumulations, which will be very much diminished before another month; and some seasons, as the former, the whole face of the declivity is without a patch of snow. On the north side there lies a vast field, which never dissolves. At about 1000 feet below the crest, it breaks up, but continues in slips and scattered masses to the bottom of the dell, or where the stream finds a regular channel at 13,500 feet; and where the cliffs are steep, it occurs at a much lower level. The day before I left the pass, the dissolution of the snow was very rapidly going on, the great field was subsiding and separating from the rocks against which it leaned: vast rents formed during the night, and the surface became soft and full of cavities, but winter would be back before any great effect was produced. When the rainy season gives over at the middle of September, the line of snow is not at its greatest distance from the sea till October, and it may not occur till November, if the weather is clear. Humboldt's measurement of the altitude of the snow in the parallel of Mexico, was made in November, we cannot then but be astonished to see our Indian surveyors and the Cognoscenti of the west disputing about the boundary, as concluded in May and June! I made some experiments here with barometrical tubes, to ascertain the quantity of error likely to be involved in the worst constructed instruments of the kind, by comparing the height of the quicksilver, freed of air by boiling, within the tube, and that in a tube simply filled. The extreme error in the latter, amounted to .130 of the barometric scale, equal to about 200 feet, and if the air had been less hurried, the difference would not exceed 100 feet.

It rained till 3 o'clock of the 13th, and the Rol people arriving, I took leave of the pass. We were in rain and fog immediately after, and I was again prevented from taking barometrical observations. At the head of the dell, which we quickly reached, the sun came out, and we once more enjoyed the genial warmth of his rays. Our course was in the dell over the snow, and at dusk we encamped at an elevation of 11,800 feet, amongst a very rank jungle of plants, arborescent Rhododendrons and Juniper. The stream of the pass is here very considerable, and finally emerges from the snow, which is almost continuous from the head of the dell, and in some places is 70 or 80 feet deep. The road lies over it, the current only at times appearing. The snow thus accumulated can never all dissolve, being detached from the mountains as fast as it collects, it becomes eternal by its mass. The whole of this night it poured down in torrents, but the change of climate was comfortable to the feelings, although I would gladly have foregone it to ge rid of its disagreeable accompaniments. There were myriads of insects which came out of the thick jungle, and extinguished the candle, and tormented me in a thousand ways. The snowy zone, with all its rigours, was better than this. The rest of my journey I shall relate in a few words; having comprised the general features of country and climate, in describing the Shatool, and which, being new ground to you, is likely to be more interesting than that perpetual subject the glen of the Pabur.

The morning of the 14th was fair, but foggy: Thermometer 50°. As we had to cross a part of the Shatool peaks, by Sheear, and drag up a wet tent by a tangled and very difficult road, it was doubtful if the camp would reach the village on the Seepon; and I resolved to halt at the line of forest on the opposite side of the range, and go on to Jangleeg, the following day; my object being to get on elevated ground before the turn of summer, and continue there till my time allowed me no choice but that of a precipitate retrograde. This was a dreadful day's journey, beginning with misery and ending in misfortune. The rain set in immediately on leaving camp, and did not cease till 4 o'clock. The road is not to be described. I drank freely of spirits without feeling the effects. At noon we crossed a part of the ridge at an elevation of 13,600 feet, the barometer being here observed under shelter of a projecting rock. We had taken a wrong direction in the thickness of the fog, but were nearer the level of the pass, and in endeavouring to keep on the same line, we became beset with difficulty and danger, and after wandering about for an hour, we got into the road, and at half-past one were in the crest. The barometer stood at 18.200, answering to an absolute height of 13,800 feet, the wind blew very hard from the south, and it rained. There we were, utterly miserable, and it was great exertion to put the barometer up. Two patches of snow only remained, and these were thawing so fast that they would disappear during the night. Vegetation was scanty on the ridge, which is level, and slopes off very gently to the sides; being flat where it is crossed, the snow must lie long, and the soil was scarcely animated. A very striking difference was observed between the vegetation of opposite faces, that looking to the E. and S. E. preserved its luxuriance to within a few feet of the top. A natural line defined the boundary in the strongest shade that it is possible to conceive. On the S. W. aspect, or that by which we ascended, the sward had been thinned by rock and want of nourishment, some hundred feet below the top. The variety of plants is also much greater on the side of the range facing the Himalaya eastward, than on its opposite exposure, This may be in part accounted for by the form of the masses, for it seems to be a pretty general law with respect to these mountains, that their west and north-west faces are cliff-sided, while the slope looks south-east. This is owing to the dip of the stratification, and we can trace a line of inclined planes sheeted with snow, beyond Jumnootree, which also shows a precipitous and sloped side. These are the very crests of the Snowy Chain, and cause a very imposing appearance at a distance, and viewed in the near prospect we are lost in wonder at the regular colour and calm surface of one side, and the ruggedness and perpetual destruction of the other. After taking a dram, I made the best of my way below, the wind blowing furiously, and the rain falling in large drops as we descended, till we were lost in thick mist, and thicker darkness. At an elevation of 13,400 feet, I was astonished to find myself in the midst of extensive plains of the richest pasturage, crossed by cairns of loose stones and running streams. No park in the south of England could vie with the verdure at this extraordinary height. A little further on we surprised a large black bear, who looked at us, and made for the rocks. At 3 P. M. I was at the trees, which are here oaks, and begin at 12,000 feet. We could neither strike a light, nor shelter ourselves, but I determined to wait for the camp. The first sound we heard was the clamour of the

Rol people with part of the tent. They came whistling along, armed at all points against the weather; cheerful in adversity they knew better than to ponder on it, and striking fire they lighted their pipes and began to dance, advising me to make for the village. To this I at last agreed, and fortunate it was for all of us. I suffered much from rheumatism in my knees while descending, and latterly was dead lame. The villagers were acommodating, and I was soon by the side of a large fire, which with dry clothes and new milk was in my present state a greater luxury than India could offer to the capricious tastes of her indolent sojourners, I mean those only who feel no inclination to pass the threshold, and meet the unknown privations and pleasures of adventure. I sunk into sleep, and night brought the unwelcome news that the whole camp had lost the road in the mist, and could not be heard of, but I was comfortable enough, and had not much cause of complaint, although put to shifts. I passed the night on a floor above the cows, but I shall not attempt to describe the situation I was in, or the sensations excited by a host of thousands. The 15th came, but it was sunset before the camp made its appearance. The height of this village, Tangno, is 9300 feet, or nearly the same as Jangleeg. The scenery in the neighbourhood is well known to you, and I can add nothing new or interesting. The mountains are stupendous, more from the abrupt form of their masses, than from actual elevation. The Changseel Range is a fine object; the part of it directly opposite to this, rises some way beyond the line of forest, and as this observes a pretty regular level, I should assign 12,500 feet for one of the summits, and 13,000 feet, at least, for another. They are covered with green sward to the last, and crowned by tumuli of stones, sacred to the Deotas or Gods. The mountains rear up as we approach the source of the Pubbur, but they break into rugged cliffs. One of these, opposite Jangleeg, is 14,000 feet, but all vegetation ceases, for a great way below the summit; patches of snow lie in sheltered situations, but the open exposure of the loftiest points was bare rock.

The morning of the 16th was lovely, the clouds

resting on the sides of the hills, the snowy tops above them appeared insulated in the air, shining with dazzling splendour at the rising sun, as if beyond the region of storm. The thermometer was 50°.5. While I was regaling myself with the sight, I was told that the Sango of the Seepon had been carried away during the night. I suspected deceit on the part of the Jangleeg people, whose habit and repute are not the most orderly; but on further inquiries, the truth came out more unfortunate than the report. A party of Koonawurees were crossing, and the sango, being frail and crazy, broke down, and one of them was drowned, or rather swallowed up. I immediately gave orders for the repair of the bridge, and moved in expectation. I found one end of the spars resting on the surface of the water, but sufficiently secured by a rope, to make the passage safe. This stream is frightful to look at in the rainy season, and the confluence with the Pabur appears like a line of breakers. A slip here is not to be recovered On the bank stood the unfortunate brother of the lost! I turned from the sight of the overwhelming torrent, and arrived at Jangleeg. The distance come to-day was only two miles, but the afternoon was rainy, and I halted for the night. This is your favourite spot, 9400 feet above the sea, and you could scarcely make a better choice, surrounded by hoary tops of incredible height and grandeur; perpetual agitation at their feet, and perpetual repose on their summits; their sides inaccesible, and there vegetate the gloomy pines. Jangleeg, although the last and most elevated village in the glen, is even the best: the seasons are similar to those of our high northern latitudes. The summers are warmer, if we calculate the power of the sun, but the shade is ever cool. The winters are far more rigorous; July and August is midsummer, but it falls short of the temperature of my native town Aberdeen. Before and after this the nights are chill. June is a pleasant month, when clear, but 48° is no great degree of heat for the mornings. September feels cold, but if clear, is a delightful month. After the 20th the thermometer falls as low as 44°. October is very cold; nights frosty. Winter now commences, and lasts till April, when it often snows at this advanced period. The rainy season, at this elevation, is gloomy, but not unpleasant, and, as far as I can judge, is healthy. Fires are always necessary at night, and are often comfortable in the day-time, when the temperature falls to 60°. The medium heat of July and August is 65° for the day, and 57° for the night, but when it rains, the thermometer seldom rises above 62°. The mean temperature of the climate here appears to be 43°, or equal to that of the 59° of latitude, but the soil is more fruitful here. The superior altitude of the sun's rays, and the moisture of the air, cause a quicker developement of vegetation, and the crops only suffer from the severity of winter. Let us compare the above with the stagnant atmosphere and mouldy heat of the plains, and I am sure you would rather choose our abode in the midst of the clouds, than one below them. Notwithstanding the unusual duration of the last winter, the effects have been less grinding than I expected. The wheat and barley had not filled out, but I found no difficulty in getting supplies. The Batoo and Phapur were heavy, and although yet unripe, they had begun to gather it in, to preserve it from the bears. The circulation of your money has been of much benefit to the country, while your friendship for the people has given them confidence, which will be turned to the advantage of future travellers; but they must behave themselves, whoever they are, since they will be judged of by the standard you have left, and these highlanders are free in thought and action. They know not the value of a bar of gold, but they must be paid for their labour. There is no slavish devotion about them, and amongst their own superiors they prefer returning a blow to pocketting the affront. I lodged here in a temple, about 150 feet above your camp, under the chestnut grove, or rather walnut. I do not wonder at Major Close being enamoured of the spot, and I trust he will yet derive the pleasure he has so often contemplated from it. The barometer was here 21.560, and the temperature of the air 63°, now delicious in August. The snow had forsaken the tops of the nearest peaks, which are above 14,000 feet, but beds in reserved situations descended to near the level of the village. Hitherto I have not observed any line of perpetual snow, so that it is still a desideratum where it actually occurs. On the 17th I brought my camp to the extremity of the forest, in the dell crossing the Pabur by the snow. The day was brilliant, and allowed me to make barometrical observations. Grain crops in this neighbourhood attain the height of 10,000 feet, and were formerly extended beyond this. The fields are of Phapur, and thrive freely. Batoo also grows in this zone. I took great trouble to discover the region at which trees arrive at their greatest size, but they seemed not to be subject to that uniform advance and decline, which we might suppose to be an effect of elevation, where the climate is distributed in strata one above another. The finest trees seem to vegetate at a height of about 10,500 feet, but we often find them within a few feet of the boundary, where they disappear altogether. I measured deodars of 13 feet circumference, and 140 feet high, at more than 10,600 feet, where also were oaks of eight and nine feet girth. The largest tree occurred at 11,000 feet. It was fifteen feet. Birches of nine feet, at a little higher; but it is necessary to observe, that the zone of the birches only begins at 10,500 feet, and ceases at 12,500. The pines, which form by far the largest proportion of the forests in every place, and thrive under a great variety of climate, show their best growth at a general height of 10,300 feet, or between that and 11,000, in the glen of the Pabur; but if we take a medium of a large space, and include the whole Alpine belt hither to the Himalaya, we may assign 9000 feet for the general limit of their size, as we find them on Mahassoo Range. Beyond 11,000, forest grows thinner, and trees are of less girth and height, but now and then a solitary trunk of the largest class occurs. A little further on they are visibly more slender, fewer branches, and crooked; at 11,500 feet, many have their tops broken off by lightning or the winds, and groups of bare poles are to be seen cleared by the lightning, but commonly they disappear suddenly, while in full perfection. I could trace very little progressive decline, and they often vanished, I would say, without a cause, remaining full grown to the last. The heat to-day felt uncomfortable, although great part of the road was at a general elevation of 11,000 feet. The sun shone clear, and the thermometer once rose to 70°. The Pabur was still arched over by the snow in several places, and we found no difficulty in crossing. My camp was here at 11,800 feet, by which I conclude that yours at Leetee, on the opposite bank, does not exceed 11,700. The birches rise above this to the height of 800 feet, but have not pushed themselves further up the dell. They generally shrink from the mass of the Himalaya before they arrive at their proper level. We were all the afternoon involved in thick mist and light rain, of the temperature of 51°. Opposite to us was the Leetee Cascade, at times visible like a column of ice raying at the sun. On looking up the dell of the Pabur, one does not at first recognise his situation, and if the neighbouring mountains are hid in the clouds, we have nothing to indicate the bosom of the Himalaya. We forget, or rather, are unable to estimate, our own lofty level, and it is this that weakens, and, in a great degree, destroys the effect of the stupendous scenery. No pinnacle within sight rises to 17,500 feet, and the ridge that closes in the dell, above the source of the Pabur, is only 16,000 feet, so that we only see the great Himalaya under an actual elevation of 5000 feet. But there is still a grandeur in the aspect of their sharp spires, bare sides and perpetual snow, which characterizes the Himalaya as a chain of transcendent height and vastness.

The morning of the 18th was fair, but mists were floating on the sides of the mountains. These dispersed by sun-rise, and the thermometer fell as low as 43°. I had before me the best prospects of a fine day, and was stirring early, having an ascent of more than 400 feet to accomplish, to get upon the ridge of the chain that separates the Pabur from the waters that flow to the Buspa and Sutluj. At half-past 7 o'clock I took a course straight up the face of the mountains, with a view to observe the height of the mercury in the barometer at the limit of the trees, which ran up in a belt, by the edge of a chasm containing a stream of liquefied snow, rising in a break, and pass to Lee Lewar. After the usual climbing, half buried in the long rank vegetation, which, loaded with vapour, soaked us to the skin, we crossed the slippery bed of the stream, at great risk of being precipitated into an abyss. Hence, along an *almost mural face* of the channel, where it was necessary to support one side by a stick, and hold on by the bushes and tufts with the other arm, the finest rhubarb met us at every step. At ¼ to 9 I sat down on the trunk of a birch-tree, the last of the group, and found the barometer 19.100, it having been 19.700 at camp; the height of the spot is 12,500 feet, and the birch-tree measured four feet in girth. A few twigs crept a little beyond this. I still ascended on a ridge of rock and soil mixed, till I came in view of the gap which leads into the valley of the Seepon. Vegetation ceased here, and cakes of snow lay in several places. There was a level here, and the snow, being screened, remains long on the ground. All beyond this was rubble and snow. The barometer was here 18.800, equal to 13,000 feet, but Juniper rose 400 feet higher. I was on the northern exposure, and the rocks reared up like a wall, and defied either the rest of snow or plants. I hastened down again, and followed the Pabur to its source, labouring under the greatest debility and depression. As I mentioned before, I found it utterly impossible to go on. Here, pitched on the margin of a lake of perpetual ice, the banks of which are enamelled with flowers, I shall now, my dear Lloyd, bid you adieu, and if there is any thing in the sequel of the route that you may wish to hear, I shall begin again, but the charm is lost, and how can I make up the deficiency now? But I will write again if you bid me, so take my best wishes in the meantime, and believe me,

Affectionately, yours,

J. G. GERARD.

END OF THE FIRST VOLUME.